AF062406

The SERGIO TORRES Story

FROM THE BRICK FACTORY TO OLD TRAFFORD

Pitch Publishing
A2 Yeoman Gate
Yeoman Way
Durrington
BN13 3QZ
www.pitchpublishing.co.uk

© Sergio Torres and Juan Manuel López, 2013
Reprinted 2014

Translated by Iván Molina Corona and Christopher Ornée

All rights reserved. No part of this book may be reproduced, sold or utilised in any form or transmitted in any form or by any means, electronic or mechanical, including photocopying, recording or by any information storage and retrieval system, without prior permission in writing from the Publisher.

A CIP catalogue record is available for this book from the British Library

ISBN 978-1-90917-876-2

Typesetting and origination by Pitch Publishing.

A Brief Introduction. 7

Chapter 1 11

Chapter 2 56

Chapter 3 124

Chapter 4 137

Chapter 5 180

Chapter 6 207

Chapter 7 227

… to Lena and Luna
… to Raúl, Mabel, Rosana and Diego
… to Fernando, Celia, José, La Nena and grandmother.
… to Cristian Levis
… to John and Mimi
… to Russell Martin and Jazzy
… to Luisina
… to Jorge Timoner
… to Mario Stilman
… to Pezza
… to Keith
… to my good friends Agus, Gusi, Luis, Pata, Ari and Nico
… to the tricolores
… to the wolfpack

In different ways they all helped us. Marked our mistakes and offer their support. Thank you is not enough.

A Brief Introduction

"The fear of dreaming should be penalised. The prohibition of dreaming should be punished by the strongest sanction possible."

THE INTENTION of this book is to tell a story, but that's not the main idea behind it. Using the course of a person's life as our backdrop, we want to talk about dreams and utopia, about sacrifice and suffering, about values and willpower, about ability and hardship, along with the hundreds of other untold tales which we haven't uncovered yet.

It is a true story, covering a part of Sergio Raúl Torres's life. While working at a brick factory in his native Mar del Plata (in the province of Buenos Aires in Argentina), he dreamed of becoming a professional footballer. His destiny suggested otherwise, which is why he had to either accept his lot in life, or find the key to fulfil his dreams.

There was no other option but to take a chance and take a break from the monotony of his life. Aged 22, and with just 300 dollars in his pocket, he left behind his comfortable lifestyle, and travelled to England in search of his dream. He set off with much trepidation, without a home to go to, and a non-existent grasp of the English language. He went against the will of many, and with very little support, but he tried his luck, and ended up playing at Stamford Bridge against Chelsea, in front of 42,000 spectators, and then at Old Trafford (fittingly nicknamed the Theatre of Dreams) against Manchester United, a game followed by 75,000 fans in the stands – and millions watching on television.

Not content with flicking the ball over the head of German international Michael Ballack, he did the same thing again to Chelsea striker Didier Drogba, and found himself playing on the same pitch as world-class players such as Andrei Shevchenko, Claude Makelele, Frank Lampard, Ashley Cole, Lassana Diarra, Rio Ferdinand, Patrice Evra, Carlos Tevez and Wayne Rooney.

In between times, he had experienced some of the most unusual things imaginable. He lived wherever he could, and with whoever would take him in. He discovered that life is like a big wheel that turns and turns. He learned that you have to make the most of the time when you're at the top, while remaining aware that – when you get back round to the bottom – you have to keep plugging away and hope that the wheel starts turning once again, mindful that it can't be impossible, as you've already made it to the top once before.

His main virtue was that he dared to dream. He turned his dream into an art form, leaving everyone in no doubt that the word "impossible" should be banned from the dictionary. A regret of this author is that while writing these paragraphs, Sergio has continued to write still more chapters in his career, and continued fulfilling new dreams. For a long while, the ending of the book remained uncertain as a result of the delay.

The process of writing this book took maybe a little longer than expected. That is because the contract – never signed – between the protagonist and author only had one line: Proceed with the project only when you want to. The clause was self-evident, to the point of being elementary. There is no point of doing it without conviction.

Moreover, from here on in, Sergio's future is as uncertain as anyone else's. The one thing we know for sure is that he will continue to dream. Other dreams await him, because – all in all – dreams are what keep most people going. To dream is to live, and – what's more – it's free, in a world where it seems that we are almost at the point of paying just to say "hello". Dreaming is a way of getting by. It is a way of keeping going. In between the time dedicated to football and to his family, Sergio also dreamed of immortalising his story in print.

This book, it should be noted, does not conform to certain formalities of others. The path of Sergio's life, when all is said and done, doesn't conform to that of most people either. This book is not a biography, nor does it belong to any particular genre of literature. It was written purely to fulfil another dream – nothing more, nothing less. Sorry for the inconvenience.

Juan Manuel López

Chapter 1

"Wretched are those who are afraid of taking risks, because they will never be disappointed, nor be disillusioned, nor suffer like those who pursue their dreams."

"ATTENTION PLEASE. Aerolíneas informs that the flight to London ..." A female voice was announcing the departure. And that announcement, completely normal to everyone else, became an unmistakable one deep down inside him. The message was clear. There was no room for doubt. There was no turning back. Giving up was not an option and it was time to make way for the madness that was about to begin. Was it nonsense? That was how he was made to understand it. Best case scenario, it was a utopic idea. For Sergio Torres, who wasn't capable of measuring utopias or madness, it was only a dream. It was what he had been yearning for since he was very young. This was the beginning of the path to the Theatre of Dreams.

The Sergio Torres Story

The previous day, in Mar del Plata, relatives and friends saw him off without understanding it too well. They wished him good luck because that was what they had to do, but alongside their voices there were also un-trusting gazes. Several questions came to mind, some of them implied, while others were expressed exhaustively with different words: Is he doing the right thing? Isn't it quite risky? Of all people *he* is doing this? He has always been shy. What will he do to cheer himself up? And if it goes wrong? How is he going to make it? What will he eat? Where will he sleep? Doesn't he realise he's a little old for this? Is he conscious of what he is trying to do? Has he gone mad?

He felt that, from this point on, he would be labelled many different ways – "really mad", "slightly mad", "adventurer", "immature", "dreamer". He would even be called an idiot by the most sceptical. The decision was already made. He would only focus ahead, like a trained horse, fighting against the headwinds. He would accept the support, pats on the back or the odd prod if necessary. He had passed the point of no return.

For more than two years he had been scraping money together to pay for the flight. It wasn't long until the departure bell would ring. He was minutes from setting his dreams in motion. The plane to England was fuelling up and he was about to get on and try his luck as a professional football player.

Chapter 1

It was his biggest desire: to play professional football. And the United Kingdom seemed to be the place where the dream would come true. Destiny had made its choice. Sergio Torres was already 22 years old and this would mean that it could be the last chance to climb his mountain, to know its heights. It was like deciding between all or nothing. Although his biological clock could still label him as young, his football clock was running down. And football, a business where years are money, wouldn't give him another opportunity. He had to take the risk because there was no other way to cure his disease.

It was a huge task, of course. The surrealistic scale used to measure the outcome was tipped entirely towards NO. He didn't have much cash, he didn't have a place to live, he had no contacts and no club, he hadn't had a notable football career, he had never played professionally, he wasn't receiving any praise from the press, he had no way to support himself, he wasn't considered a "young talent" and he didn't even know how to speak English – in the five years he had studied the language in high school, he copied during the exams because he was not interested in learning another language.

He had been told there was a magic train that only passes once in a lifetime. But in his life, this mysterious machine had not even appeared on the horizon and he wasn't willing to wait for it.

He decided to go off alone to look for that long-awaited locomotive. It was time to take the other fork. He was taking the daring initiative and rejecting waiting passively. He was confident he would find that train in another station, even if it was risky.

The goodbye

His mum, Mabel Delfina Suárez de Torres, preferred not to think about the departure of her "little boy". She wasn't happy, had problems sleeping and was dominated by fears. Those fears, which were also feelings, blinded her every so often. A mother's heart tends to react in that way. They have special hearts. And they are understandable hearts, very rarely criticised. "Mum, relax. I'll be back in three weeks," Sergio told her, understanding her pain. It was a comment to calm her heart. A lie to save time until it grew accustomed.

His dad, Raúl Oscar Torres, reacted in much the same way. Although he had to admit that his son was going in search of his big dream, it wasn't easy for him either. He was already missing his son even before arriving at Ezeiza International Airport.

Sergio's sister, Rosana Mabel Torres, condemned him: "You won't last more than a month in England." She justified her words saying that her "little brother", hardly two years younger

Chapter 1

than her, was very family oriented, didn't know how to do things for himself and didn't even do the washing-up at home. That is why he would be back so soon. Rosana, in spite of her prediction, supported Sergio's project like few others. She was his number three fan, after mum and dad.

His last night in Mar del Plata was strangely divided into two parts: one goodbye with relatives (at home) and another with friends (in a pub). Both were very brief, since he still needed to pack his bags and prepare himself for the "conscious madness". Both meetings shared a similar topic of conversation: this madness. Questions were repeated tirelessly and answers were avoided because they made no sense. He was reminded again and again, as if he didn't know: "You are going to a different country, very far from here, with almost no money, without relatives or friends, without speaking the language, with nothing." Fears were on special offer at the shop, and it seemed like everybody had bought one for him to take to London.

These were not days for thinking. It was better to think about nothing.

Ezeiza: the departure bell

The heart should know things that the mind is unaware of. After all, many of the questions that were occurring to him in those moments had no reasonable answers. In Ezeiza, Sergio's mind was not an oasis of reason and was filling with doubts and fears. Every minute of waiting meant a new question that was basically discouraging.

A nearby calendar indicated his departure date: 7 November 2003. In a popular newspaper (*Clarin*) the headlines of the day reported that Roberto Lavagna, the Minister of Economy, wanted to increase the consumption of goods, and that the countdown had started for the match between River Plate and Boca Juniors, at the Monumental. The paper also mentioned that the Prince of Spain's wedding announcement had become the focus of attention in Europe. None of this interested him in that moment ... He looked at his passport, trying to find things that proved he was heading for his dream, but the cold paper of the passport only told him what he already knew:

First name: Sergio Raúl
Surname: Torres
Date of birth: 11 July 1981

In Ezeiza, Sergio awaited the departure of the flight to London's Heathrow Airport with only a suitcase and scarcely 300 dollars in his pocket. His intense love for football made up for his shortage of both luggage and money. If it would be enough or not didn't matter anymore.

There was another problem, already clearly admitted. He couldn't speak English. The prev-

Chapter 1

ious days, while running back and forth amid confusion, he grabbed a book he had used during his first year in the high school called *The Project One*, and put it into his suitcase. He also found a dictionary to take with him (they always help, he thought). And Gusi, one of his best friends, aware of his linguistic deficiency, wrote down for him the most important expressions. He also loaded a diary into his backpack to record day by day the details of his hopeful adventure.

Utopia management
In Mar del Plata, the city that witnessed his birth, growth, suffering and happiness, Sergio Torres divided his activities between studying, working and playing football. He grew up in El Coyunco, just at the entrance to the Sierra de los Padres. There, in the open country, he was always known as El Patito, son of Pato Torres, and his future seemed obvious: work and maintain the brick factory, the pride of the family, that was about 400 metres from the house.

As a youngster playing for Quilmes de Mar del Plata, he kicked the ball around just for fun. At just six years old he was already seen running around the sports club on Avenida Luro, making it clear what his true ambition was. He also competed in paddle tournaments, listened to rock-and-roll and Cumbia (the first CD he bought was by Leo Mattioli) and he liked cars just like his dad,

The Sergio Torres Story

especially Chevrolets. He was hyperactive, but his only true passion was football. Soon after learning to walk he made, together with his dad, a goal using the bidet and the toilet. For him everything resembled a ball. He discovered TV to watch football matches. He learned to read, to be able to read football magazines.

He always went to the factory. When he was young, just to play, and when he was older, to work. He helped out with whatever: grinding clay, cutting, organising and moving the bricks, picking up wood with the trucks, wetting the ground, etc. It was dirty work and tough, especially in the summer when the ovens made the high temperatures unbearable. In the winter it was also hard because the warehouse was open and you could get the flu in a second because of the cold.

Working with the rest of the employees, most of them relatives, was nice, although the days were long. His father Raúl, part owner with his uncle and his brother, paid Sergio by the hour. 'Borromeo' (what he called Sergio referring to a character from *Calabromas* who never behaved) wasn't favoured. He worked long hours like everyone else and had to work just as hard as all the others, but sometimes you could see him weaving in and out of the bricks with the ball. This was inevitable.

His father's desire was always that his kids would study to be accountants. Nobody listened

Chapter 1

to him, but Sergio at least tried, taking and failing the entrance exam. It was obvious it just wasn't his thing. Not even destiny, which sometimes is harsh, wanted it for him.

He subtracted accounting from his list and the football road, although he hadn't given up, wasn't easy either. The two best known clubs in Mar del Plata, Aldosivi and Alvarado, were interested in him but never asked him to join. It was at this point, already a bit tired of rejection, he signed up to study physical education. Why? He liked kids and he liked sports. The profession seemed to be the perfect combination of his interests, similar to his sister, who was studying to be a master gardener.

The first two years were full of difficulties and in the third year things got more complicated, so he left studying having received a tempting offer – Banfield contacted him to play in Torneo Argentino B, a national amateur league.

They offered him 400 pesos or 400 patacónes per month. A 'patacón' was a pseudo-currency that the State used to pay public workers and suppliers and was like an emergency bond. It was fake money, disguised. Crisis money. But for him an achievement – he played football AND they paid him. His life, for a year, was divided between practice in the morning and work at the factory in the afternoon. In his mind he was already making it happen. The seed had been planted.

The Sergio Torres Story

While he was saving money he also tried to put together some of his best plays with Banfield to make a DVD. With his little technological knowledge he wanted to create an amazing video to show to whoever, some foreign club or even to an Argentinian one, although in the local climate it would be more complicated. He wanted to be a professional football player at all costs, against all odds, without fear of what anybody would say.

His age and his personality weren't too helpful. He was already 22 and was too timid to go head on and too embarrassed to take shots, almost always preferring to pass to a team-mate when he could have triumphed. His insecurity made it difficult for him to make decisions but alone he managed to slowly build a great video. Although he wasn't a stand-out player, his performance in the midfield with Banfield gave him plenty of options to choose from. The idea was simple – giving it all he could lose nothing.

Day after day his obsession grew. Something, some feeling, told him he could go far. He had seen a kind of light that only the mad seem to perceive. Outside voices, however, said it was only a fairy tale – beautiful, but impossible. How, at 22 years of age, out of nowhere, could you think of becoming a professional footballer?

Having finished the DVD and with a bit of cash saved up, he managed to meet up a few

Chapter 1

times with Alejandro Giuntini, former defender for Boca Juniors, who had contacts in Europe. In this way he took another solid step forward but the dissonance sounded even stronger and the question got longer. How, at 22 years of age, out of nowhere, could you think of becoming a professional football player, and in Europe?

During one of these meetings he handed Alejandro the video. He said he was a winger but could be effective in any midfield position, and that he shot better with his right foot. These images, almost monotonous for him at this point, later ended up in London in the hands of Julio Alexaniser, fellow Argentinian and acquaintance of Giuntini, and soon they ended up in the possession of Roland, a British football agent from Cameroon. The situation was as strange and extravagant as it was fantastic and unbelievable; a simple video, edited simply by a nobody, was in England and being passed around.

Roland took charge of getting the video to various teams although, as expected, it was rejected by most. However, Third Division Brighton liked it and they agreed to give Sergio a trial.

Meanwhile, 'Paisa' (the nickname given to Sergio in Quilmes, referring to the fact that he lived in the country instead of the city like the majority of his team-mates) had gone to try his luck with the amateur club Deportivo Madryn

The Sergio Torres Story

(a team located in Patagonia) that was trying to qualify in Torneo Argentino B. However, he was there hardly two months.

Giuntini called him to tell him that somebody had taken the bait. Sergio, happy and scraping together whatever he could from wherever, raised enough money for the trip to the other continent. He had to go for it no matter what, risking what was for him a fortune, trying not to analyse it socially or economically.

His parents were frozen by the news. They weren't expecting something like this since Sergio was really close to his family and because he had never showed much courage in facing various challenges. First they figured he probably wouldn't end up following through, that it was like a childish game, but they soon rejected this possibility. They were extremely frightened. They had already freaked out when he took off for Puerto Madryn and they heard of him sleeping on the ground on discarded mattresses. In that time they were so alarmed that his dad tried to head down every weekend to help him out however he could. His mum also went at times.

"What are you doing here, mum?"

"I've come to clean you up a bit."

Sergio Torres, beyond his dreams about the ball, wanted to see other worlds and cultures, and demonstrate that he could be worth something. This was another of his fights.

Chapter 1

"Why are you going to England? You've got everything here; your house, work, money, your family and friends. There you don't have anything. Please tell me what more you need here and I will get it for you," begged his father, attempting to stop him.

"I only need the OK from you guys."

Once the unconditional support from his family was obtained, Paisa boarded the plane, and on arriving in London he had to get in contact with this Roland guy.

Welcome to London

8 November 2003. The plane landed at Heathrow Airport. "Welcome to England" he said to himself in English, deciding that he had better start trying to understand a bit of the language. He was in the UK, in Great Britain, in Europe, in London, whatever. It didn't matter. He couldn't believe it. From Mar del Plata to London. From "hola che, cómo estás?" (hey man, how's it going?) to "hello, nice to meet you". The road, which he had travelled so many times in his dreams, had now finally been done while awake.

His feeble knowledge of the language kept him quiet and he had no idea how to behave in this arrival to an unknown land. It wasn't surprising though. Luckily, a sign bearing his last name saved him: at the exit he saw a man holding up a card that clearly read "TORRES". Slightly reluctantly, he went over to the man and tried to understand what he was attempting to tell him in his strange accent. There was no hope. His English was horrible.

> *The only thing I can say are the colours and that my name is Sergio, which doesn't help at all. I'm a disaster. This is what I get for not paying more attention in school. They also told me that before every introduction I should say: 'Hello. Nice to meet you.'*

Sergio Torres had an ace in the hole for these circumstances: making use of the universal language of the eyes. They always helped him out in these times. He knew that in our eyes there are dozens of words and dozens of feelings understandable for any human being regardless of nationality, and that looks are tools to build indestructible bridges for concepts to be carried to their destination. He used to believe that there are few things you can hide when looked in the eyes.

"To know somebody, it's not necessary to do more than look him in the eyes," his father used to say. He also knew that gestures, added to the game, help to form a double blow. Like a great fighter, Sergio put in practice both tactics, and figured out that he had to wait over in the corner for at least ten minutes. Why? Well, he wasn't too sure yet.

Chapter 1

Who's this guy? Is he just a taxi driver who's taking me to meet with Roland? Will it be expensive? How do I pay him? Am I the 'Torres' on the sign? And if it's not me, bad news.

The man, still unfamiliar, tried to explain what they were doing there, but Sergio couldn't decode even a portion of what he was saying. During this ten-minute lapse, Julio Alexaniser arrived, the Argentinian acquaintance of Alejandro Giuntini. He breathed a sigh of relief to hear a familiar language.

"This is the Roland that you have heard about."

I don't know why we didn't begin with this information. He could have just told me his name. He didn't need to drive me mad wondering who he was.

"This is your agent here in England, from Cameroon. He's going to take you to the trials and help you with whatever you need … He's going to take you to his house. Don't worry about anything. Only two people fit in his car, so I'm taking the train and we'll see each other later to talk more and get organised. Sound good?" Julio explained. Sergio nodded suspiciously, but he had no choice.

The Sergio Torres Story

Home, not so sweet home
After travelling for an hour and a half, they got to Roland's house. Sergio wasn't able to see the neighbourhood because it was already getting dark. He wanted to catch everything he could, to the last detail. If life is really a collection of moments, he felt that he should take advantage of the present to not have any regrets in the future. Thirty minutes later, Julio Alexaniser got there and started to explain the situation, how he should act and what steps they were taking.

"This is Roland's second house. His two brothers live here. One is married. Two friends also live here. You're going to stay here too … As you know, the trial starts next week … I've got to leave you here with them and head home, which is pretty far from here, north of London. Relax and we'll be in contact. Everything will be alright."

Immediately after Julio's explanation, the occupants of the house appeared: all from Cameroon and not one of them knew even a little bit of Spanish. To make matters worse, they communicated together in French.

Thank goodness I don't have to pay for a hostel. This way I'll be able to support myself a bit longer in Europe. I don't know how long I'll stand it here. This house is weird. Six guys from Cameroon and me. I don't understand what they say. I know, everything can't be perfect.

Chapter 1

Sergio introduced himself timidly but courteously ("hello, nice to meet you"), just like his parents had taught him. Since it was getting late, Roland took him up to the first floor to show him his new room. Paisa paid close attention to the details, but sleep was taking him over and he decided to rest.

I thought I was going to be alone in the bed, but about an hour later I started to feel the bed moving. One of the guys came into the room, laid down next to me and, like it was nothing, told me to move over saying something like "scoot over, I sleep here too". I freaked out and started shaking. I didn't respond because I was the new guy and because a paralysing fear took over me. He wanted to kill me. I couldn't believe it but I couldn't get him out. It was then I realised I had to share the bed with him and that I was always going to have to. To top it all off, he was fat, hairy and snored like a bear.

I laid there looking toward the window, frightened and wondering: 'How did I end up here? What was I doing sleeping with this guy? I was fine in Argentina. Thank God I had everything I needed: work, family and friends.'

I didn't catch a wink all night because I was worried ... and for other reasons.

The Sergio Torres Story

England, day two
The problems that he had earlier ignored or put off were now coming to light and he was jotting them down in his diary. The first night, in which he didn't move a muscle, didn't do him any good. His distress began to agitate him. *Who are these Cameroon guys? What if they try something?* His suspicion didn't allow him to think straight: *What if this is all a big lie?* And his fear, not wanting to be excluded, was growing: *What am I doing here if I was fine at home?*

Sergio wasn't exactly satisfied in Mar del Plata. He simply put up with it, which wasn't the same as being happy. His soul wasn't content. He was going the easy route, comfortable with the routine into which he had fallen. He went around knowing he could have a normal life without any big problems and, whatever "they" might say, he wouldn't be affected. He went around thinking he would make a difference; plant a tree, write a book, have kids. He went around with the dull sensation of knowing what was coming and that he was missing what he really loved and was searching for: to be a professional football player.

Paisa, in self-defence, emphasised that there aren't many people who think they should live how they want, instead of conveniently, because life is short. Since he had left home, he had been putting his feelings before reason and logic. He had come to terms with having to conquer adversities and be

Chapter 1

guided by his heart because, sometimes, thinking too much was counterproductive.

Diary. 9 November

Since I got home really late, I still wasn't familiar with the neighbourhood. I'm in a small town, Norbury, about 50 kilometres from the centre of London. I was tired today because I hadn't slept at all. It was impossible with the guy sleeping next to me. But, in spite of my fatigue, I went out for a walk in this new world. This place is really strange. I didn't see a single white person in the whole area and on top of that, with my long blonde hair, it seemed like everyone was staring at me like a fish out of water. I was shocked and I suppose they were pretty surprised to see a guy with long blonde hair.

The different sides of waiting

Everything wasn't going exactly to plan; not necessarily a bad thing since exact plans sometimes get in the way of happiness. His life was a mix of unpredictable experiences so he figured that it would be foolish to expect it to be predictable. Inside, he decided to not get more depressed than he already was. If right now he was suffering, perhaps later he would be glad. He tried to focus only on his objective, his dream, and wait for his chance; always waiting, again and again.

This is definitely what he thought it was about. It seemed to him that a big part of life consists of waiting. You have to wait for your dreams, for vacation, you have to wait for love, for a better job or for a raise. It was up to him to make the wait shorter and easier.

"Life is a big waiting room." (*Diez años después*, **Los Rodríguez**)

With the passing hours, Sergio Torres was drawing conclusions continually. In these moments of self-reflection, he remembered the words to different songs he had heard in Argentina and jotted them down. In certain places there weren't any red lights. You just had to take the road, just happy to be moving but never attempting to finish.

Sometimes, of course, he had to walk the coals: it started to get dark around 4pm and the cold froze you to death. At the house, he was extremely bored. At night, he read English books to learn a bit more of the language. In the morning, he watched TV for the same reason. He still didn't understand much, almost nothing. He barely spoke with the other inhabitants of the house. Only one of them bothered to talk with him: one of the guys from Cameroon who looked like Fido Dido, the Seven Up mascot with the crazy hair. He was friendly and tried to help him, but the language barrier hindered his good intentions.

Chapter 1

"Food is another thing. They eat white rice with red beans every day. Every once in a while, they might eat pasta, but little more. In the fridge there aren't many options," Sergio wrote in his diary, letting out his frustration.

Getting started

Finally the big day arrived: Monday, start of the week, the training and the trial. It was time to demonstrate he was ready to be a professional. It was the moment to spend all his time doing what he liked to do, or rather, time to exhibit his toughness to the max.

Up to this point, his stay in England hadn't exactly cheered him up, but, if he looked back and saw only the negatives, he also had the option of looking forward.

As the training ground was far, they took Roland's luxurious Mercedes Coupé.

I'd love to drive this machine. Someday I'll ask him, speaking in my horrible English. But it doesn't matter, even if I pronounce it well, I doubt he'd let me take it out.

An hour and a half later, they arrived at the right place, where Brighton trained; a team fighting to move up to the Second Division, now known as the Championship in England. The weather didn't help much. It was cold, rainy and windy.

The Sergio Torres Story

It wasn't exactly a fairy tale. When they got out of the car, they went directly to the bar until the manager, Mark McGhee, arrived a few minutes later. He was introduced immediately to Paisa, who only got out "hello, nice to meet you", a phrase he already had incorporated well into his vocabulary and which was his only greeting.

In the locker room, while some of the players came over to give him a simple welcome, others just ignored him. He, however, gave a simple "hello" to all as either a greeting or an answer. The atmosphere seemed friendly, but the looks, universally understood, said something different. This sensation was confirmed when he realised that he was in the part of the locker room where the veterans were.

What an idiot! Starting off on the wrong foot, he thought, and he quickly moved to the section where the younger players, and the others trying out, were changing.

> *This place is incredible. Brighton's training ground is fantastic. The pitches are beautiful with some amazing grass. There are four excellent fields. I really can't believe it.*

During the first day of the trial there was physical and ball work ("I was always at the back of the queue because I didn't understand anything the coaches were saying," he added to his diary) and

Chapter 1

30 minutes of football, which he was looking forward to, although it wouldn't be easy.

Diary. 17 November 2003

They barely passed the ball to me. They looked at me and they went the other way. The few times they passed to me there was immediately someone down my throat. I went flying after my first two touches. A bald guy from the other side was on me the whole time. He had a dirty look like he was going to eat me alive. I don't think I'll ever forget his face.

Not easy at all
English football was tougher than he had thought; very physical and tactical. Sergio Torres was confident in his technical skills, his able right foot and his natural South American style acquired on the pitches of Mar del Plata. He was also sure of his toughness. However, during his first week in England, his team-mates passed him like bullets and he couldn't hide it. They were like jets, he remarked. Their speed was unreal and running into them was like hitting a wall without wearing a seatbelt.

In Argentina he just waited for the ball to come but here he had to go and get it. At times, the people who doubted the success of his adventure began to be right. It was impossible just to arrive in England, with very few resources and many things against him, and become a professional football player. It was a utopia or just plain stupidity.

He did know one thing for sure: dreams shouldn't be criticised. One should be punished for fearing a dream and they can't be forbidden. It would be a crime with a serious punishment. He didn't want to be condemned for such a transgression. Furthermore, you would think that dreams were made to come true and, if they exist, it's because we should be capable and free to fulfil them. We should at least try, without ever being reproached.

Sergio Torres had the instinct from the very first whistle. He wanted to erase the word "impossible" from the dictionary. In spite of the blows (physical on the pitch and psychological away from it), he had to continue the week of training, trying to give it his best; going head on in everything he did so that, at the end, he wouldn't have to ask himself, as many others have to, what would have happened if … ?

The good and the bad
After the first five training sessions, Roland spoke with the manager, Mark McGhee, in an English still incomprehensible for Sergio. Luckily Julio Alexaniser was around during those days to translate for him.

Chapter 1

"The manager told Roland that he liked how you played and that he wants to see you another week."

"But wasn't this what we had agreed on?" asked Sergio, surprised.

"What?"

"Supposedly, it was a two-week trial. This is what we had agreed upon in Argentina. I was coming here to train two weeks for Brighton."

"No, it ended up being a week."

"You tricked me."

"Nobody tricked you. I'm sure it was a misunderstanding. Forget about it for now and be happy because the manager wants to see you another week. This is what's important and the only thing that matters because he liked your performance."

Sergio couldn't hide being upset at feeling a bit betrayed. The emotions of the last few days added to both the positive and negative feelings. The words of Julio Alexaniser, however, comforted him a bit and took away the sting. "The fact that he wants to see me again is good because he could have just said 'no' after the first week," he wrote in his diary, which played the role of counsellor and was where he unloaded his experiences.

The trial: round two

Monday 24 November 2003. He seemed to just be a few yards from his dream. He could see it on the horizon. If everything went well, he would sign a contract with Brighton to be a professional football player, reaching his first peak. He was going step by step up the climb, which was easier than he had imagined. He had a place to stay and free food, and so could survive on the little money he had. He managed to get an agent who was taking care of him. The trial, which hadn't been certain, materialised. His play, which didn't seem too popular, was being praised. His age, which he thought was an obstacle, didn't matter. He was only five or six days away from signing a contract with an important club in a major level. In English football, even the lower division teams are professional and are run like businesses.

His happiness dispelled any need or inconvenience. The stone he was pushing daily was rolling into position and he started to cheer up. Now the optimists were right; doing is believing.

Sergio started to recognise that much of the "I can't" was only in his head, that sometimes reality lies and that everything is not as it seems. Little by little he began to realise that he needed to throw away the book of formalities. At the same time, you could see inside him an invisible power that had the power to dissolve any problem, even to nothing. Willpower? Could be. Who knows?

That Monday, the 24th, began with an obstacle to get around. His only pair of boots had broken during the last training session on Friday. At the

Chapter 1

weekend, he had asked Roland if he could please buy him some new ones, of any brand.

"Luxury is vulgarity." *(Un poco de amor francés. Patricio Rey y sus Redonditos de Ricota)*

Luxury was insignificant during his stay in London. It didn't matter which boots, it was only important to have them for the second week of training. Roland, able in these situations, told him that he would go to the club and get a pair from a team-mate which he did. However, they were two sizes too small.

Diary, November 24th, 2003

Roland went to ask somebody for some boots for me. Being shy with these things, I didn't want to take part because I was embarrassed about it. He brought me some boots that are two sizes smaller than I'm used to, but I put them on anyway. I curled up my toes inside and clinched my teeth. I didn't have the guts to tell Roland: 'They don't fit me, can you bring me others?'

During practice I was in pain and looking forward to taking them off. They were killing me! What a relief at the end! They left me with six blisters. Right now I'm soaking my feet and I think I'll stay like this all afternoon.

The picture of a poor guy with his feet destroyed moved the African and he decided he could dig into his pockets a bit, so he took Sergio to a shop and bought him a new pair of boots. They were the cheapest, in fact, but this didn't matter.

> *I was pleased to be free of pain while playing, although my feet still bothered me.*

He started to get to know his team-mates, and they began to trust him more. His feet started touching the ball more and these feet treated him better, allowing him to play his style and distribute the ball well. He still couldn't speak English although he had been there for 20 days. His shyness didn't help with words, but since football is not understood through languages and races, the training sessions started to go better. So well, that the managers came over to tell him he would be playing a match as a reserve.

> *Unfortunately, the match was postponed and I was left wanting.*

The decision

Friday was coming and, with the new day, he would know the final decision. How could he sleep? How do you wait for an answer that could be sweet or sour? How do you tell yourself to not get nervous, knowing that you are playing in the

Chapter 1

final? He tried, he sacrificed and he had done his best every day. This was enough for him and it tranquillised him, but again the same idea came to mind: conformity is not happiness, they're not even related.

Various scenarios passed through his head, which was full of a mixture of possible conclusions. He was sweating despite the freezing cold, which proved he was extremely nervous. The official dictionary of Argentina says that "transpiración" [sweating] in the winter means "nervous", and that "frío" [cold] in the summer means the same conceptually.

The good thing during these moments of sweating and expectations was that he had nothing to regret. He simply had to keep his gaze firm despite what happened.

The manager met with Roland to give him the decision, which he did coldly and methodically. He didn't accept suggestions nor did he try to explain himself. Getting directly to the point, he said:

"He's a good player, but he doesn't have the speed or the strength to play football in England."

The frustration
His world went to pieces. The manager's face turned into a gun and every one of his words was like a bullet. This answer had always been a possibility, but nobody is ever prepared to

suffer. There are no schools where they teach you to fight pain or how to prepare yourself for disappointment: how much can words hurt and how deeply? What is their value? Mark McGhee's painful words to Roland hurt. They impacted him and left him an unforgettable scar.

The disillusion was offensive because everything (or almost everything) had made him think the opposite as the last five practices had gone so well. Sergio wasn't the only one disappointed. So was Roland. Now the Cameroon businessman wasn't smiling. He looked upset.

> *He's not happy with me. He says I didn't play like in the video he saw. I don't know, it's what I think he's saying. I really don't know what I'm going to do.*

It is tough to admit the battle was lost or that the dream wouldn't have a happy ending. How do you surrender when you're not ready to give up? Hours later, the sentence was still stuck in his head: "He's a good player, but he doesn't have the speed or the strength to play football in England."

He wasn't ready for the adventure to stop. He wanted to keep dreaming or at least try to. He could find another way. Why not? There's more than one way to reach a destination. In Mar del Plata you could take a boat, a train, a plane, or even highway 2 or 11. Why not try it?

Chapter 1

Why, why and why?

The pessimist in him said it was because there weren't any reasons to do it. But the optimist responded that maybe there were.

"The heart has reasons that the brain will never understand." *(El final es en donde partí, La Renga)*

"I'm going to fight and I'm going to triumph in English football."

"Dad, I don't want to go back and don't want them to tell me: 'Look. That's the guy that failed in Europe.' I don't want it to happen."

"Look son, nobody's going to call you a failure. Nobody. A failure is someone who doesn't even try and you tried. If you want, stay there and we'll support your decision, and we'll help you however we can."

The conversation between father and son decided it. Sergio Torres couldn't imagine himself going back to Argentina. A specific memory bothered him – in Mar del Plata, while he was watching a game from the stands with his dad, he heard everyone yelling "failure" at a player who had returned from Europe without success. It bothered him what everyone else could think about him coming back. He had a complex – his feelings scared him – but he also had a virtue; his feelings were stronger than his reasoning. Sergio wanted to continue fighting in some way, but how? This was another point he still hadn't analysed. He wanted to battle for the important things in his heart. The problem was though, the little money he had was running out.

> *I spent a bunch of cash to get here. The trip was extremely expensive. I can't give up so soon. I'm going to fight and win.*

His family and friends were convinced he would return. That the trip had ended. They were waiting to give him a big hug and show him their support. They realise that the dream still wasn't dead. Nobody had killed it. It had only gotten shot a few times.

"There is madness, with no name, date or remedy, that is not worth curing." (*Locuras,* Silvio Rodríguez)

In his feeble, poorly pronounced English, he managed to ask Roland if he could stay a few more days at his house and, since he was already there, if he could organise another trial with anybody, hoping he could use his contacts (if he really had any). The African unconvincingly agreed.

Chapter 1

Diary. 29 November 2003

It's really strange for me the fact that I'm going to spend my first Christmas far away from home. But, luckily, I know I have the support of my family and friends. They know that I'm following my dream of being a professional, to make a living doing what I like best, which is playing football.

Back to waiting

The days and the weeks passed. Roland didn't get him even one trial. Almost every morning he said he would get him something here or there, but never specified. He was lying. Meanwhile, Sergio Torres tried to stay in shape although he was quite unfit for what English football required. He had prepared himself a training regimen:

I get up every day at nine o'clock. After eating breakfast and watching TV a little while, I go for a workout. I dress warm since it's freezing cold in the morning. The field I run on freezes. The back garden of the house is next to a school with a grassy field which the kids use during break time, and I've already learned at what time it is. So, while they are in the classroom, I know I have two hours to work out.

I do 100-, 200- and 400-metre sprints, going as hard as I can. After running, I put different obstacles, like cans, sticks and branches, in a line to weave through with the ball. Sometimes I spend 30 minutes kicking the ball in the air and trying to control it with each foot. I play motivating games. I have a stopwatch which I use to time every exercise and do it faster the next time. In the afternoon, I run more and do more ball work.

* * * * *

There was some non-football related stimulation to his life in England which helped kill the routine: communicating with his loved ones on the internet. It was an incredibly gratifying way to feel closer to them, even if virtually. He had to walk five blocks to where there were a few internet cafés. This was his lone pastime. It was like a source of energy two times a week. Because of his economic situation, he couldn't connect more often (it cost £2 per hour, which was a lot for him). Sometimes he wouldn't even buy a bottle of water after his workout.

One day, close to one of the doors of the house, he saw a £2 coin on the ground.

When I saw it, I thought 'this would be great to get on the internet for an hour', but I couldn't pick it up. It wasn't mine. I've never even stolen a sweet from the shop and I'm not starting now.

Chapter 1

Furthermore, it belongs to somebody who lives here.

The next day, the coin was in the same place, in clear view, and it kept calling my attention because nobody had grabbed it.

I waited one more day and I thought 'if no one picks it up, I'll take it', so I took it and thought 'nice', because now I didn't have to pay for one hour of internet. I went directly to the internet café and said to the man who worked there 'one hour internet'. I gave him the coin and he started to laugh. After a moment, he said: 'That's two pence!' It was a 2p coin. I had never seen one. I thought it was £2. I got really embarrassed and realised immediately why nobody had picked it up. It was the first and only time that I've stolen in my life.

Peligro – danger

He was getting incredibly bored. With timid but repetitive gestures, he was continually asking Roland to go out and do something like going into the centre of London (Norbury, where he lived, was 30 minutes from the English capital), but it never happened. One afternoon, surprisingly, the African appeared and told him to get dressed because he was going to take him somewhere in the car. He happily put on his best clothes and they left at 6pm. Roland's first stop was at a friend's house, and then he said they were going to stop and say hello to another friend, at a garage. "OK, no problem," Sergio said.

> *When we were entering the garage, underneath the train tracks, the darkness caught my attention. We entered through a half-broken chain link door. There were three or four garages next to each other and you could see the train passing over every now and then. We got out of the car and he introduced me to the owner of the garage, dark skinned and friendly. There were two other people there, who were working on the engine of a car.*
>
> *After being there for ten minutes, a tall black guy arrived. He walked right past me to the office where Roland was. On seeing Roland, they started arguing immediately and then they both came out. I stayed next to the car that was being repaired. They were arguing very heatedly and the big guy (called 'Panda', I don't know if it was his real name or his nickname) pushed Roland, who gave me the keys to his car, and I understood that I needed to hold on to them. They kept arguing and went back into the office.*
>
> *Five minutes later, the huge black guy came storming out and directly at me, yelling at me to give him the car keys – I really didn't understand, but imagined it's what he was saying. Roland yelled "no!", and since I didn't*

Chapter 1

give them to him, he pushed me against the car they were fixing. I started to get scared. I went to the other side of the garage, leaning up against other half-fixed cars, and he came at me again grabbing an immense wrench on the way, the biggest one I'd ever seen. He yelled, demanding the car keys and raising his right hand as if he was going to rip my head off.

Roland, three yards away, insisted I didn't give him the keys. I didn't know what to do. With his left hand, the guy tried to grab the keys from my right hand. I panicked and managed to throw the keys to Roland. 'Panda' didn't like this and lifted the wrench to hit me. Here I thought 'this is it', because he would kill me if he hit me with that thing. He changed his mind and slugged me in the chest, throwing me against the car behind me. I hurt like crazy. Then he turned around and took off with Roland again.

I couldn't stop shaking. I looked around the place and heard the noise of the train above, and told myself 'it's destiny'. It was like a movie. I really thought I could die there. If they killed me, they could easily make me disappear since I didn't have any family there or anything. Nobody would be asking about me for a while.

I couldn't wait to see the black guy leave. After about ten minutes, Roland appeared and said: 'Let's go home.' I was still shaking. In my bad English, the first thing I said was 'what happened?' He said he was sorry and explained that 'Panda' wanted to take his car in exchange for money he'd loaned him and never got back. At least, this is what I understood.

I immediately felt like going back to Argentina. We got home around 10pm and I went straight to my room. I felt horrible but I couldn't tell anyone. If my parents found out, they'd ask me to go straight home. Sometimes, the desire to return to my country is immense.

Destinations

Not every situation is comfortable and desirable but you can take something from all of them, even something insignificant from something extremely negative. While he was waiting for news from Roland, suffering from instability and missing his loved ones, Paisa continued training alone, however and wherever he could. During these uncertain days, he also took a day to visit the famous Big Ben, Buckingham Palace and Tower Bridge, doing a bit of sightseeing around London. It was like a story book for him to be among these important landmarks that he had only seen on TV or in magazines.

Curiously, the thing he liked the best about the day was ending up in Julio Alexaniser's house that night, because he was able to use the computer until three o'clock in the morning. He chatted with family and friends, and felt close to home listening

Chapter 1

to some radio stations, from Mar del Plata, via the internet. It is amazing how sometimes the little, mundane things can be so gratifying.

A week later, Roland told him about a new opportunity. Destiny was giving him another chance. The club was Woking, from the Conference, the fifth division in England. The African took him there the first day to introduce him to the manager and players. For the trial, the next day, Sergio went alone.

> He told me he can't always take me because it's a bit far from where he lives, so I have to go by train. He marked on the map where I had to get off and where I had to wait for another train towards Woking. In all, it's about a two-hour trip.

Another opportunity was presenting itself and he couldn't waste it. He simply had to try again and remember the motto "trying is not failing". He needed to attempt it without hesitating. He figured that in some things you have to arrive at the end or die trying, never being satisfied with halfway.

He imagined that the training sessions would be just as tough as with Brighton, even though it was two leagues lower. His suspicions were correct. Making his minimal experience in British football count, he was able to surprise everybody with his play, even sticking out at times and impressing the manager.

His bad fortune began to turn around and his mood along with it – his frown changed to a smile and his sad eyes became happy – causing a notable change in his persona.

The wheel keeps on turning
His family was still worried even after hearing about the new opportunity. They had reasons: their "little boy" was living alone for the first time, at a house in a 'questionable' south London neighbourhood, with unfamiliar Africans that speak French together and English with everyone else, and who have different habits from him. "Who knows what he's eating or where he's living," they wondered in El Coyunco.

"Ask the owner of the house if I can come and stay for ten days, nothing more. That way you won't be so alone and we can spend Christmas together."

"Are you really coming to England?"

"Yeah, to spend New Year's Eve together."

"Are you serious? I can't believe it. How are you going to do it?"

"Don't worry about that. I have some money saved and it's enough to pay for the flight."

"You're not pulling my leg, are you?"

"No, son. I've been saving. It's not much but it's enough. Now, please ask the African if it would

Chapter 1

be OK if I stayed there, because otherwise I won't have enough."

Sergio was extremely pleased about the news from his father. Now the wheel had made a full circle. He had had to really get down to be able to get back up. The positive things happening with Woking and his father's pending visit helped to fight his loneliness, a powerful and unexpected rival.

His loneliness before the visit, something that didn't fit on either side of the scale, weighed heavy on him, although sometimes he needed it and required it, while at other times he fought for it to go away. Often it was like a friend with countless virtues, but sometimes it was like spending time with an enemy.

> *Soon after, I politely mentioned to Roland that my father wanted to come for just ten days, and if it would be possible if he slept on the couch, since it wasn't being used at the moment, plus anyway he wouldn't be a bother as we would be out and about all day in London or some other place. Smiling he said that he could stay: 'Yes, no problem.'*
>
> *I can't believe my dad's coming to see me. I feel more alone than ever and his visit will really help me keep fighting.*

Ten days later he talked with his father again to finalise the details.

"Son, I bought the ticket. Make sure everything is OK at the house."

"Yeah dad, don't worry. I talked with Roland and he said it's no problem that you come. You don't know how happy I am. When he gets back home, I'll tell him it's for sure."

He was super excited. He waited for the African all afternoon to tell him that his dad had got the ticket, and that he would be coming in five days. He was happy. His mood had made a 180-degree turn.

At nine o'clock that night, Roland showed up in his car. Sergio was so happy that he went to give him the good news before he even entered the house.

"What? What? What?" he surprisingly started yelling; a cruel reaction after hearing the news.

> *He gave me a look I'll never forget. I thought he was going to eat me alive. He told me to go inside. I went to the dining room and he came in with his brother, who was in charge of the house. They both started yelling at me, and saying that I was crazy for telling my dad he could come, and that there was no room in the house, etc, etc.*

Once again, like so many times during his stay in England, he felt like the world was falling to pieces, but this time the pieces were falling

Chapter 1

harder, more violently. His head began to shake from side to side like it was trying to reject what was happening. Just listening to Roland hurt. He didn't understand the reproaches and ended up exploding: "Go to hell!"

He ran to his room crying and his tears blurred his vision and his thoughts. Roland came up behind him with the phone, speaking to Julio Alexaniser, telling him that "the kid's crazy and wants his dad to come for ten days". The telephone seemed alive, jumping from person to person.

"He told me 'yes' before and now he's saying 'no'! My dad already bought the ticket. He can't do this to me! Now my dad won't be able to come because he doesn't have money to stay in a hotel. Why did he tell me 'yes' before?"

"Relax Sergio, relax," urged Julio Alexaniser.

"I can't relax Julio! Plus they're yelling at me like madmen. This hurts a lot."

"Relax, everything will be alright. If you go mad, it'll just be worse for you."

Roland continued yelling. In the noise, languages and accusations were mixing with the tears. The angry voices only added to his frenzy and he blew up again: "Shut up, you son of a bitch!"

"Bitch? Me a bitch?"

"Yeah you! Go fuck your sister!"

The African raised his tone, getting more violent. His last line had been too much. End of story. There would be no sequel. Although the Spanish that Sergio was speaking wasn't Roland's mother tongue, he understood perfectly, ripped the telephone from his hands and without leaving time for apologies, he threw him out of the house. There would be no argument. He didn't want to see his face again. In less than five minutes, the wheel had spun back around and Sergio Torres was once again down in the depths.

That night Paisa packed his bags, knowing that the next morning he would have to leave for who knows where. Usually, when he was feeling down he couldn't sleep. That night, his last, was no different. All the thoughts in his head made it hurt. His legs hurt, his arms, his back, his soul … The play was over and the curtain had closed definitively, but there was no clapping or cheering; only worry and anguish.

At seven o'clock in the morning, he grabbed his few belongings and took off to look for another place to land. Before leaving, he found a pen and paper to write a note to Roland and the other occupants of the house. He left it on the table in plain sight, in his simple English, without resentments, thanking them for all their help. Then he left, closing the door behind him and knowing that he was also closing opportunities and possibly his dream.

After walking a few steps away from the house, he turned around to look at the place where he

Chapter 1

had spent the last month of his life and wanted to take a picture to remember. The only person he saw around was a street sweeper about a block away. He called him over.

"Can you take a picture with the front of the house, please?"

The man kindly agreed. After it was done, Sergio Torres started walking. Where? Somewhere. Or nowhere. It was the end. Or was it just AN end? Because they say that every ending is a new beginning.

Chapter 2

"There is a driving force more powerful than steam, electricity and nuclear power: the will."
                                        Albert Einstein

A CASUAL ENCOUNTER between two mothers would be the connecting thread that would weave another story. Sergio Torres found out, during his stay in England, that on the other side of the Atlantic his mother had re-established contact, after many years, with Cristian Levis's mother. Cristian had been a team-mate of his when he played for Quilmes in Mar del Plata, during those times when they just chased after the ball, just trying to kick the round thing and make everyone smile. They grew up together playing football, hide-and-seek, or whatever, but the passing years had distanced them and they hadn't heard anything from each other for quite some time. "Right now my son is trying to play professionally in England," said

Chapter 2

one of the mothers. "My son too!" commented the other, surprised by the coincidence.

Coincidence or destiny? The two ladies exchanged their sons' e-mails so they could get in touch in the UK.

Cristian was staying in Paddington, right in the centre of London, half a block from Hyde Park, one of the biggest parks in the city. From there, if he wanted to, he could run to Buckingham Palace in half an hour, although the Guard would detain him immediately for obvious reasons. He was staying at the house of his agent, Jorge Timoner, which he shared with two other men: a Swiss, Marco, and an Italian called Alessandro. Also staying there, thanks to Jorge, was a fellow Argentinian, Pablo, who was also trying his luck in the football world. The high rental prices in the English capital are the reason why the flats are usually shared by so many. Reducing expenses was the key to getting by in a place where the cost of living was so high.

Julio Alexaniser unexpectedly knew Jorge Timoner well: both Argentinians and friends, they played a similar role in player representation. Now, plan A for Sergio Torres was to live at Jorge's with Cristian. There was no plan B. Plan C? Go back to Argentina; a possibility that grew with every passing day. Julio Alexaniser called his friend to see if Sergio could stay at his flat, since he had no home or money.

Jorge agreed, and Paisa, with the permission granted, got on a train from Norbury towards the centre of London. Getting kicked out of Roland's house had destroyed Sergio's planned path. The coincidence with Cristian, added to the incidental friendship of Julio Alexaniser and Jorge Timoner, provided him with a new route, although he wasn't interested in having to decide his direction in the moment. He felt, for the first time, that he wasn't obligated to choose his new life's path, because he was confident he would be able to get by while he waited for its completion. In his diary, he had written down the famous Spanish poet Antonio Machado's suggestion that Joan Manuel Serrat made popular in a song:

"Caminante no hay camino, se hace camino al andar." – Traveller, there is no path. The path is made by walking.

The new drawing board
Julio Alexaniser called him to give him Jorge Timoner's address, who was on holiday in Andorra and would be back at the beginning of January. It wasn't easy for Sergio to find his new place. He had only been in London once and had never been around Paddington, but being disoriented wasn't a bad thing at this point: asking for help and walking around, he learnt.

Chapter 2

During the 30-minute journey from Norbury to the centre of London, he tried to find some answers to the questions he had been asking himself since before he left home. When he had time to kill, he attempted to find a way to create a beneficial relationship between feelings and reason. On one side, he didn't want to be a hopeless romantic who only feels and doesn't think, but on the other side, he wanted to be an intellectual that had no need to consult his heart to resolve complicated situations. His mind was ready to live new experiences in every moment. It was ready to fight untiringly with little or no certainty. It was strange: he had convinced everybody how important his dream was, but, at times, he needed to convince himself of what he already knew.

When he arrived in Paddington and had walked around and interrogated whoever crossed his path, Sergio saw Cristian Levis's face in a lonely window, realising with relief that he had finally found the house. The actual reunion – before it had only been a virtual one – was emotional and comforting. The hug they shared was one of welcome, happiness, strength, support and friendship. Sergio needed it but he didn't really know how much. He thought immediately about the power of hugs, how they are capable of transmitting hidden forces. Later, with more time, he investigated the subject and discovered, in a book by the Uruguayan Galeano, a doctor from Barcelona whose opinion was that the first desire of a newborn baby is to be hugged. The infant doesn't wonder if the other will be uncomfortable with the hug because it assumes that they want the same – welcome, happiness, strength, comfort, support and friendship – as Sergio and Cristian had found.

Cristian Levis was home alone with Pablo. They were introduced at once and, from the first moment, started to get along well. The Italian and the Swiss, like Jorge Timoner, were also away on holiday. It was the end of December, time for Christmas and travelling.

> *This is another world for me. I'm living in the centre of London, about 100 metres from the city's biggest park. It's a beautiful place, with luxurious houses; a fantastic neighbourhood. Being here I realise why everyone is impressed when they visit this city.*

New Year's Eve celebration, New Year's Day of mourning

It was the first time Paisa had celebrated Christmas far from Mar del Plata and his family, and he was experiencing mixed feelings with extra melancholy thrown in. That cold night, Santa's night, he had dinner with Cristian and Pablo. The three of them raised their glasses at midnight and

Chapter 2

went out on the street to see the fireworks. They had no gifts coming. It was obvious that the old, bearded man dressed in red wouldn't be visiting these three vagabonds.

> *To our surprise we didn't see a single firework, firecracker, nothing. I don't understand why. I had the same explanation for everything, whether it was true or not: 'It's just another culture.'*

As there was nothing to see outside, they went back in and turned on the TV. Meanwhile, they took turns using the only phone in the house to call their loved ones back home. They decided to go back out and have a walk in the park, but froze once again and hurried back to the cosy flat.

Seven days later they got together again to celebrate New Year's Eve in the same way, but the difference was that, this time, there were fireworks. He explained it the same way: "It's just another culture here and they must only celebrate on the 31st."

On 1 January like three English gentlemen, but dressed humbly, they left the flat early to take a long walk around London. These three English gents, hungry like dogs, visited historic landmarks, learnt different customs, mixed with the locals, enjoyed special moments and laughed. Their legs were their vehicle, as their half-empty pockets didn't allow them the luxury of using even public transportation.

When he got home, Paisa got on the internet and was surprised to immediately see a strange message from his cousin Horacio asking him: "Where are you?" Not even "Happy New Year". What followed was even stranger: "Your dad has been calling you for four hours and he can't get a hold of you."

"But what's up? Has something bad happened?"

"Talk to your dad."

Cristian Levis was using the telephone. Worried, Sergio asked him to hang up immediately. He already was getting the chills, expecting the worst.

"Hi," his dad barely squeezed out from Mar del Plata. The loud man of many words was short of words this time and speaking quietly.

"What's up? Did something happen to mum?"

"Mum's fine. So's your sister Rosana, but your cousin Sergio …"

"What's up with him?"

"He had a car accident this morning …"

"…"

"He died."

Sergio Martin was his cousin, but even more so, he was like a brother to him. They were only five months apart in age and had lived only 300 yards from each other. From infancy until they

Chapter 2

were teenagers, they spent time together playing football, riding bikes, making tree houses, and they even went to the same school. They shared the type of moments that are locked forever in the box of memories, and that never go away. When they were older, times changed and they began exploring together the nightlife of Mar del Plata. They each had their own group of friends, but Sergio Torres would go out one Saturday with his mates and the following Saturday with his cousin. The relationship was so special that this select group, comprised of 'Cabezón' Matías, 'Pelado' Andrés, Leonel, Rulo, the other Matías and Leo, accepted him.

There are no words to express how he felt. It was a devastating blow. The rejections and the problems he was having in England were insignificant compared to this tsunami. Sergio went to be alone in his room for a few hours. He couldn't stop crying. He had cried many times already in Great Britain, but this time his tears were overwhelming, and he was inconsolable. Silence speaks louder than words and Cristian and Pablo, seeing him silently weeping, understood perfectly. There were no words to express his pain. He only came out of his room to call home again and talk to his father.

"I'm coming home, dad."

He already had a return flight for 3 January but had been willing to miss it in order to stay in Europe to play, to fulfil his dream of playing professional football. He had this dream in sight, conscious that if he tried, he could see it through, but the news about his cousin changed everything. His Theatre of Dreams was crumbling down. Sadness was taking over. He preferred to take the flight and head back to Argentina to be with his family.

"I'm coming home, dad."

"Do what you like, son."

"I'm coming home. That's it."

"Do what you like. If you want to come, come, but think that you're not fixing anything by coming back to El Coyunco. It's madness here. Think that you won't make it for the funeral or the burial, and think about how much you've fought to get where you are now. If you return, forget about having another opportunity to live your dream."

"I don't know what to do, dad." Crying, Sergio thought silently for a moment, breathed deeply and continued: "We were born together, we grew up together and we did everything together. It just doesn't seem fair that he's going away and I can't even say goodbye."

"I understand son, but like I said, when you arrive it'll be too late. But do what you want to do. You know that mum, your sister and I will support whatever decision you make."

Confusion was entering Sergio's head, taking the place of hope. Life, the unjust and implacable

Chapter 2

coach, had made the decision and would accept no arguments. It was disconcerting. Once again, his mind was unable to agree with his heart. It was almost impossible to accept without thinking and, at the same time, extremely difficult to think without feeling. Sergio picked up his pen knowing that writing would help him to get things out.

I have no team here, I've had two months of shit and everything is going badly. I can't solve anything in Mar del Plata either. When you're dead, you're dead. If I stay here, what will my family think for not being with them at this time? If I go, I won't even arrive to say goodbye.

Take the flight or stay in England? It was not a new option but it now had a different impulse since he had no time to delay the decision; the flight to Buenos Aires was leaving in less than two days. He turned back to his trusty surrealistic scale, weighing each side the best he could, but it was useless and seemed just plain stupid this time.

What would he have preferred?

He knew how proud his cousin had been that he was following his dream. This alone would defend the act of staying in the UK and not going home. He went back in his memory to remember last time they had talked on the phone, three days before the accident. He saw now that this conversation had been his goodbye, and thinking back, he realised he would never forget him and, in this way, would partly keep him alive because forgetting is the only way for someone to truly die.

First gear

After heading in reverse, things started moving ahead and gaining speed again. What had been an obstacle had been overcome, and Sergio decided to remain in England. On 3 January he didn't go to the airport and the reservation was cancelled. Now he really couldn't go back to Argentina because he had no money. He was tied to England and his dream of being a professional footballer. Had it been necessary to accumulate reasons to stay in Great Britain, he now had one more: his cousin.

That day, 3 January, he met Jorge Timoner, who had finally returned from his holiday. The next day, the other two flatmates also came back; Marco, the Swiss, and Alessandro, the Italian. Everybody together in the same space was sure to cause some friction.

> *The Swiss guy is not too happy with us, but he's right. We're in his house. The Italian, however, doesn't mind. He's pretty easy-going. As long as we don't make a mess and we clean up after*

Chapter 2

ourselves, there's no problem. Jorge and Marco had an argument right away. He assured him we would only be staying a few days but, as we still don't have a club or money to go anywhere, these few days have turned into almost a month. I can understand why he's pissed off. But anyway, I think we're conducting ourselves pretty well.

The passing weeks were not easy for him. Thoughts of his cousin appeared at any hour. Every day an anecdote or a conversation they had had came to his mind, which was acting independently, unearthing memories whenever it wanted. His subconscious was even more uncontrollable and witnessed fierce battles. Paisa fought it one on one: sometimes winning by a small margin, sometimes drawing, while at other times suffering a heavy defeat.

The relationship with Jorge was very positive from the first time they shook hands, and this helped him not to sink in the storm he had to sail through. During those days, he started going out at night in London to clear his head. He went to the popular clubs, which were small and where you had to be on the guest list to get in. Sergio had no money nor did he consider himself special, but Jorge's contacts allowed him to enter even when it cost £20. Dimitris always seemed to come along on these nights. This friendly guy from Cyprus quickly became chummy with Sergio. During his stay in Europe, Paisa had already hung out with people from Cameroon, Argentina, Switzerland, Italy, England and now Cyprus. Without knowing, his head was being enriched by information from various cultures. The experience was also teaching him …

> *It's doing me well going out at night to distract myself. There are a lot of small, fun pubs here. Luckily, 'Jorgito' has a lot of contacts. Otherwise, it would be impossible to get in. We almost always go to a place called China White, where Jorge knows the owner. It's strange for me to see the ladies in short skirts or tiny dresses when it's four or five degrees below zero. There are also a lot of drunk women throwing up in the street. It's normal to see guys like this in Argentina, but here, I see more women like this.*

Despite the few but fun nights out, the focus remained on trying to get picked up by a football club. The best thing was that now he didn't have to do it alone: Cristian and Pablo were in the same boat and, while they waited for their chance, they burnt calories and time training together.

> *We go running every day to stay in shape and get stronger. We run in no less an arena than Hyde Park. We bring a ball and set up two goals*

Chapter 2

using sticks or whatever we find in the park. The one-on-ones get fierce and the winner stays on. As it's raining a lot now, we always end up covered in mud. The other day, covered in mud, we took a picture in front of one of the Hilton hotels. It came out great.

Second gear
Unlike Roland, Jorge Timoner was much more efficient in finding a team, and furthermore, he was doing it for Sergio, Cristian and Pablo. The club was called Molesey and was a little more than an hour's journey from London. To get there, you had to take a train to one station, and then transfer to a different line which went to the field. The trial was with a club in the eighth tier of football in England, a semi-professional team that only practised twice a week, on Tuesdays and Thursdays from 7pm to 9pm. At the beginning, it wasn't exactly what Sergio Torres had been looking for. He wouldn't be a professional footballer with Molesey, but as he had learnt, "the path is made by walking". He needed to start somewhere. You have to walk before you can run.

The three of them got on the train, expectant, anxious and nervous, to go to the first day of the trial. That morning, Jorge Timoner couldn't take them in his car, but he had arranged for the club owner to go pick the boys up at the entrance to Hampton Court station. This would save them

The Sergio Torres Story

the price of another short train ride and the trouble of trying to find the club.

When they got off the train, to their unpleasant surprise, they saw nobody waiting for them. Looking at the clock, they realised the meeting time had already passed. It was scheduled for six o'clock in the afternoon – or rather six at night, since the English winter, apart from freezing you through, also shortened the days. Sergio, Cristian and Pablo, shivering in the cold, waited in the station because there was nothing else they could do. They didn't know how to locate the field themselves and they didn't know exactly how to ask either. Luckily, 30 minutes later, a luxurious black car appeared. There were sighs of relief.

> *I sat in front because I speak the best English of the three, but I still didn't understand anything. He spoke a lot, but I understood absolutely nothing. I simply moved my head, like nodding in agreement, pretending I knew every word he was saying. I always use the same tactic: I move my head with a serious face, transmitting understanding with whatever the other person says. But this time I really didn't catch anything.*
>
> *The man took us to the stadium, showed us the locker room and we noticed immediately that we were three Argentinians changing with twenty English men. They looked at us strangely, and we were so nervous we weren't*

Chapter 2

even able to say 'hello'. That night we practised on a dark, muddy pitch.

There was enough football in the six South American feet to hide any defects and to compensate for any lack of strength in the legs. Steve Beeks was Molesey's manager and to the Argentinian trio's surprise, he approached them after practice to express his interest. Without hesitation, he wanted all three of them to join the team. The little he had seen was enough to convince him they should be part of the squad.

It was difficult for Paisa to believe. They had only attended one training session and the trial, which he expected to be long, ended up only lasting a few hours. Many times life gives us unexpected surprises, and this quick decision seemed to be one of them, but it was still hard to believe. It was like a mysterious compensation for past pains that destiny at times provides.

After hearing Steve Beeks's words, Sergio was doubly satisfied, and his damaged heart allowed a smile to be seen on his face: first, he had understood perfectly the manager's declaration, a good sign, and second, although not less important, he now had a club to play for.

The nomads
Jorge Timoner spoke with Molesey's management team to close the deal. In the meeting, there was a

disappointing revelation. The club wanted Sergio and Cristian, but not Pablo. The unexpected news was devastating to the three boys because they had prepared together, spent good and bad times together, had learnt together and would have loved to play together on the same team.

After the bad news, Pablo was unable to find sufficient strength to stay hopeful. He decided to go back to Argentina. Would it be a mistake? Choices are difficult to diagnose and this decision was bothersome because they had become like brothers, and now one of them had to abandon his dream. The physical separation was what disturbed Sergio, not the mental separation, as their days of living together in London had left hidden but permanent marks and would keep them mentally linked forever. Time and its unstoppable march is always able to discredit memory, to twist anecdotes and erase images, but it's impossible to forget the invisible impressions engraved in your soul. The heart keeps them protected.

We'll miss him.

The cards were reshuffled after Pablo's departure. Sergio and Cristian began a new stage as semi-professional footballers in England. Jorge Timoner worked out the details and managed to get them both a £150 fee per week; not much for

Chapter 2

the high price of London life, but a fortune for the two of them in those days.

Having money in their hands and a team to play for, they were obligated to look for another place to live. The situation with Marco, the Swiss, was intolerable. Sergio and Cristian left the flat that same night and, with their bags in hand, went to look for a hostel or another flat, but unluckily found nothing and returned to Jorge's. The Swiss was steaming and they had to explain to him, slowly and patiently, that it would only be for a few hours until they found another place. Marco didn't believe them and for good reason – before, they had said the same and those "few hours" had turned into a month.

Two days later, they left the unpleasant atmosphere of the flat and, back on the hunt, found a cheap place to stay. Located in a nice area, close to historic Hampton Court, the flat was new and clean. They would be sharing it with a friendly Serbian girl. Paisa continued adding nationalities to his list of flatmates.

Torres, the player

Now, more at peace having their own place and not having to deal with Marco's rebukes (fair and acceptable, but annoying), Sergio Torres and Cristian Levis were able to concentrate on their objective: playing football. Paisa, a versatile midfielder, and Cristian, a striker, made their debuts playing at home and both of them were in the starting 11.

> *We both had a strong impact on the team's victory. I almost scored, but the ball hit the post. I wanted to kill myself because it would've been a tremendous goal. But c'est la vie, moving on. The league is not too good and everybody just runs around. After 90 minutes, they were all still going like the first minute. They play at 100km an hour the whole time. No ground passes. The balls I got were clearances by the defence or 50/50s. Nobody gave me ground passes. It wasn't much like football, just sheer force and effort. Bummer I didn't score that goal, but I think Cristian and I did our part and they were happy.*

Sergio began to understand, and rightly so, that if he wanted to do well in English football, he would need to change his style of play. He liked the challenge because he would need to adapt without losing his essence. In Argentina, especially when he played as an attacking midfielder, he needed to wait for the ball to come to his feet, but in England, he had to go looking for the ball in the pack. Sergio liked teams that played the ball on the ground, making short, first touch passes if possible, constantly moving and respecting the ball, playing in a triangle when necessary, making

Chapter 2

forward passes when there's space, making hidden or delayed runs, getting back on defence or helping out in a quick attacking play, working both sides and the centre, possessing the ball, and not trying to move up the pitch at all costs as if it were a game of rugby.

He didn't like playing long ball football, hoping for something that probably wasn't there, and he didn't like waiting 90 minutes for his opponent to make a mistake. His manager wanted the opposite: sacrifice and more sacrifice. Nice to watch and helpful play seemed to be extinct there, especially at this level. Not taking risks and always clearing the ball were two concepts he needed to accept. Sergio didn't agree with his coach and thought: "Why not take risks with a little ball inside a green rectangle if I'm taking risks in life?"

He continued jotting down his experiences and reflections in his wrinkled, dirty and disorganised diary, which had been with him since before he arrived in England. He had developed a method; first, he wrote what had happened during the day – if he had time or if there was something worth writing about – and later, as a way of digesting everything, putting down what he had learnt. He didn't try to write down truths as he still hadn't found any. Furthermore, he was discovering that truth really was a big lie.

He did, however, try to record the situations that changed his way of acting, even when he didn't want to change much. There was one fact he couldn't ignore: learning more helped him realise he knew less. In his diary, words and phrases in English started appearing almost unconsciously ("England" instead of "Inglaterra" for example). This was a good sign. Sometimes, seeing so many words, he would begin to remember more song lyrics.

"I wish being brave wasn't so difficult or that being a coward wasn't worth it." (*Noches de boda*, **Joaquín Sabina**)

Nothing is impossible
The stage in Molesey, including great performances and praise, lasted less than expected and less than he had wanted: only four games. At the end of the month, Steve Beeks informed them that he couldn't pay them what he had promised. The club had no money and it would be months until they could get a loan. Sergio Torres and Cristian Levis were disappointed, but they still had to pay rent and basic costs, mainly food. They would have liked to stay longer with the club, at least as a thanks for making them a part of the team, but they couldn't. In England, just like anywhere, you can't pay the bills with just a smile.

Steve understood their problem, realised the boys were in a tight spot and felt pity for their situation. He decided to help them, doing them a big favour: he got them a trial at Basingstoke

Chapter 2

Town, a team two levels higher, where he had played and with whom he had a good relationship with the manager, Ernie Howe. The trial would last 15 days. It was also a semi-professional club which practised two times a week: Tuesdays and Thursdays from 7pm to 9pm.

"Yes, of course," they answered in unison without hesitation. They also answered using this phrase because it was one of the few that they could pronounce properly and they wanted to demonstrate how good their English was. A minute later, they admitted to each other that this was their only option.

Petty economic reasons but significant emotional incentives came together in this offer. Sergio Torres and Cristian Levis soon left the eighth tier of English football behind and took a serious step towards professional football. They were extremely excited about the chance to try out with a club in English football's sixth tier, even though they had to continue travelling by train, as Basingstoke was about an hour away from where they were living. The distance was not the problem, nor was the inconvenience. It was the cost of the trip.

> *Cristian and I have almost no money left. Luckily Jorge is keeping us fed and he just gave us a little to pay for the train. I don't think we can keep living here and go to the trial two or*

three times a week. It's complicated. Why does everything have to be so difficult?

Being signed by Basingstoke would be great progress. Sergio got out his famous surrealistic scale: the things weighing in favour were clear and what was weighing on the other side was how to survive economically during the two weeks of the trial (pay for rent and food but being able to afford the train rides to attend the practices). After careful consideration, the verdict was simple: you couldn't think about doing it, you just had to do it.

They decided to move ahead knowing that, at any moment, they could run out of cash. Thursday would be the first day, and they would need to squeeze out their best to be able to stay with the team after the two weeks. The first day, Pete Peters, the club's assistant coach, was going to pick them up at the train station to bring them to the field where their possible new teammates practised. Sergio and Cristian, still a bit disoriented in the city, made a crucial mistake arriving an hour late to the meeting point. The match hadn't even started yet and they were already losing by a mile.

There's a well-known saying: 'Never arrive late to the first day of work.' Well, like a couple of idiots, we broke that rule. And worse yet, the trial only lasts two weeks.

Chapter 2

Luckily, Pete Peters didn't seem to be annoyed at having to wait 60 minutes. He took them to the playing field and, obviously, the players and the manager, Ernie Howe, were already training.

The cold, and the fact that they weren't accustomed to it, made those nights of practice extremely complicated for the two Argentinians.

> *It's horrible. I'm trying to ignore it somehow, making myself stronger, with my head high, like saying: 'It doesn't bother me.' I look at everyone else and they don't seem to be suffering, and truthfully I don't think they are. They're like polar bears in their element. They don't even flinch. These guys are strange. Cristian and I are dying of cold. Dying! We shiver and end up looking like morons. There's one thing clear – we are the least wrapped up of anybody, but I'm not about to go out and buy a jacket in London when I barely have enough to eat.*

The field where they were training was wet due to the constant rain, which lowered the temperature even more. Immediately, the two boys from Mar del Plata went over to the manager and the players, shook hands with everyone, apologised and began to follow the movements of the other players; some physical exercises, some tactical, and at the end, a scrimmage. It was at this point that Sergio and Cristian, with their surprising skill, began to make up for their late arrival and the manager changed his opinion of them. He was so delighted that afterwards, he called Jorge Timoner to tell him he wanted to use the boys as substitutes in the match the following Saturday. Having heard the news translated by Jorge, they were left speechless.

> *We're very happy. At the beginning, the trial was going to be two weeks, but we showed up late the first day, and when we thought they were going to tell us, rightfully, to get lost, they ended up telling us they want us to play as substitutes on Saturday after only having one practice with them, or actually less than one, as we were late.*

The light that those smiles produced soon went out. The day of the match, the damn train dealt them another bad hand and, once again, they arrived late; two days with the club, two days arriving late. It was 2.20pm when they entered the stadium (they had to be there at 1.30pm). The match was at 3pm. The first thing they saw after going in was their team-mates doing the traditional pre-match warm up. Sergio and Cristian dropped their heads in dismay. It wasn't necessary to ask if they would be playing that afternoon. It was a clear deduction for anyone, and they probably wouldn't continue with the trial.

Chapter 2

They were so frustrated that they didn't even bother trying to give an excuse. It was unpardonable. They would settle for being allowed to watch the match from the stands, that way they would at least distract themselves a bit from the consternation, otherwise they could just ask to be swallowed up by the earth.

With looks of embarrassment, the Argentinians waited for the words of dismissal, but once again, their reasoning would be wrong. On seeing them immobile with worried faces, the assistant coach sent them immediately to the locker room.

This madman is sending us home in a hurry.

Still not masters of the language, they thought Pete Peters was kicking them out, however, he really was saying the opposite – he wanted them to get dressed for the match.

How can it be? Seriously? It can't be true. Is he really saying that? Is he asking us to get changed?

When they had correctly understood the message, they went running like two schoolboys to put on their shorts, socks and boots. Luck had returned to play on their side. They would end up being among the substitutes for a game at the sixth level of football in England; a fantastic situation.

But there would be more surprises. While Paisa was heading to get his uniform, they told him he would be starting.

What?

Sergio didn't understand why he would be joining the starting 11 without even knowing his team-mates or having warmed up. He didn't know why he would be playing from the starting whistle when he had arrived barely 40 minutes before the match. Furthermore, he had had less than one practice with the team and he had been late that day also. He just couldn't understand. It was impossible. It seemed like a bad joke or perhaps he had misunderstood. However, they were serious and, minutes later, he was handed his shirt proving it was real. Logic had now completely disappeared, and he was happy to find out that one plus one does not always equal two.

Together with his new and still unfamiliar team-mates, he went to the spot where they were to listen to the manager's last-minute instructions. In this exciting moment, as usual, he didn't understand anything that was said. He used the same useful technique as always; nodding his head in agreement with everything.

It wasn't my fault this time. He was speaking really fast. He said a few general things and then

Chapter 2

told me a few things. I looked at him, nodding, but I had no idea what he was saying. Not a word. I have to say, not trying to brag, I now understand quite a bit of English. I know lots of words and expressions, but the language is very difficult when they speak quickly. It all runs together.

The referee blew the whistle and Sergio Torres started his debut in the sixth tier of English football with Basingstoke Town FC, his second club away from home, playing on the left wing. He wasn't exactly sure that this was what his manager wanted but, after observing where his team-mates had set up and that nobody else was there, he put himself on the left side. It didn't go badly; in fact, quite well. He displayed his skills every time he touched the ball.

Basingstoke won 3-0, including a goal by Cristian, who scored their third after coming on to the field with 20 minutes left. While Paisa was celebrating the win with his team-mates, he was called over and informed that he had been chosen as the man of the match, all the more reason to celebrate after his debut. The award was given to him, along with a bottle of champagne, during a small presentation including the management of both teams.

We were exploding with happiness on the way back in the train. Things couldn't have turned out better. We won, I started, I was the man of the match and Cristian scored. I gave the champagne to Jorge. He deserved at least that.

Unconsciously prepared

The following Tuesday, Sergio and Cristian played their second match, this time as the away team. They drew, but the result was not important. What mattered was the decision of the manager, who had been impressed with the two Argentinians and ended up making official what was already evident: they were no longer trying out, but were playing for the club. They would be paid £150 per week, or about £600 per month. There were no negotiations. They were offered that amount and immediately agreed. They were elated until the moment they stopped to do the maths.

In spite of still being amateurs, they felt like elite athletes. They exerted effort as if it was the most important moment of their career or as if they were preparing for the World Cup. They were in their own world, finally living their dream after everything they had been through. They took great care with everything; the shirt nicely folded, the shorts and socks clean, the boots polished and tape always on hand. The few things they had needed to be protected, as they understood how much they had sacrificed to get them. Furthermore, like climbing a ladder, they

Chapter 2

had to be careful on every rung because one false step would be enough to fall.

The next match was also away, against Kettering, the team in first position in the table. Sergio and Cristian found out at the last moment the significance of the game, noticing more fuss than normal. That Saturday they travelled in a coach divided into two sections – the players sat in the back, and in the front were the team staff with 20 fans that went with them to every match – everything quite conventional, following certain universal football protocol.

> *They're our loyal supporters, called 'fans' here. The affection they transmit is spectacular. They even show support for Cristian and I. It's very impressive because, in addition to being the two unknown new guys, we're also from Argentina, whatever that can mean around here.*

This was one of the most important matches of the year for the club and Sergio would be starting once again. He was a bit out of shape and with the ball at his feet he still lacked rhythm, but he hadn't lost his technical skills, which was the key to him making up for this fact. During the pre-game he was nervous, but was also confident he could produce.

The first half finished 0-0, which wasn't bad for a team that was experiencing a bad season.

The scoreboard at half-time caused noticeable pleasure and even small celebrations among the fans, and in the locker room there were also grins. However, Sergio didn't share their satisfaction. He wanted to win – just like when he played during break in primary school or playing in the fields of El Coyunco – like always. Furthermore, they were in England, where he had learnt that nothing was impossible.

Only a few minutes into the second half, Paisa realised that winning wasn't out of the question and that they had an opportunity to come away with all three points. On one of Basingstoke's first attacks of the second half, he received the ball just outside the box, controlled it with his first touch and, with his right foot, placed it nicely in the top corner, leaving the spectators open-mouthed and demonstrating to his team-mates that you can be denied victories, but you should never stop trying.

Sergio scored a magnificent goal against the league leaders, and in their stadium. He celebrated the goal in an unusual way, but it wasn't surprising, considering how abnormal his life had been those days. When he saw the ball touch the back of the net, he took off running without knowing why. Then he ripped off his shirt and spun it around over his head, thinking about his cousin, his family, Roland and everything that had happened to him since landing in England. He continued running, now towards the other side, not knowing

Chapter 2

exactly what to do, and headed for Cristian, who was on the sideline about to enter as a substitute (a muscular problem had kept him from starting), and gave him a huge hug, celebrating what was a meaningful feat for both of them. It was a blessing that made all of the previous misery worth swallowing and, momentarily, he was in the clouds. However, the sound of the referee's whistle brought him back to earth.

We won the match 3-0. The moment I saw the ball enter the goal I went directly to give Cristian a hug, as a way to demonstrate that we are in this together and that things are going to get better. Everybody went wild with us because they weren't expecting such a thing. We played very well in the second half, loving every minute of it. As we were getting on the coach to go back, one of the fans came up to me speaking in Spanish. His name is John Gray. He told me he wanted to give me a shirt. It's last year's shirt from Basingstoke, which is cool because it resembles the ones from Boca Juniors. He also gave me a scarf. I happily accepted his gifts.

Home, now sweet home

They had income and a club and fans who appreciated them, but this money and support didn't add up to enough to cover even rent. They needed to move, but they had no idea where to, or how. In Basingstoke word got out about their problems: "The Argentinians have nowhere to live." It wasn't so important who played as a striker, what tactical scheme the manager would use or how many defenders were necessary. There was a clear message: for true fans, there are things more important than results. One exasperated supporter took the initiative of offering them his house as 'bed and breakfast' accommodation.

He had a multi-room house, like a hotel, where he rented rooms for a low price, which included breakfast. Sergio and Cristian, extremely surprised and thankful for such a gesture, accepted. They stayed there for four nights and would have stayed longer if it hadn't been for another and even more surprising invitation. John Gray, the man who had given Sergio a shirt and scarf, found the boys and told them that he had been worried by the news about their living situation and, without hesitation, invited them to live at his house.

John Gray was like an alien in this world where saying and doing rarely go hand-in-hand, and even more so because many times, instead of using words, he spoke exclusively with his actions. He was like a teacher employing one of the most effective education techniques, the example, many times not even realising that he

Chapter 2

was teaching. He gave a clear display of solidarity for all to remember and copy.

The most surprising part of his invitation was the fact that he was recently married, having tied the knot barely two months before, with a pleasant French girl called Mimi. As could be expected, she wasn't ecstatic with her husband's decision. When the Argentinians arrived at their new home, they realised immediately that the lady of the house was a bit annoyed.

> *It's great living here. It's a beautiful house and they give us everything with incredible generosity. But Cristian and I don't really know what to do at this point. We feel embarrassed because Mimi is right. It's undeniable and easy to understand her irritation. They've been married for barely two months and we've come here invading their intimacy, their love nest, their first moments as man and wife. If I was in her place I would never have accepted the decision. I also put myself in John's shoes and realised I would never have made the same offer he made us. They're both mad, but wonderfully mad.*

Not much time would pass before Mimi's face of anger would change to a smile, showing sparkling teeth and bright cheeks. It took hardly 48 hours of living together for the coldness to change to warmth.

The Sergio Torres Story

Luckily, our relationship with Mimi changed within two days of living here. Only two days. Now we are like their two 'big boys' and now Mimi is taking care of us more than John. I still can't believe that a fan, who got married two months ago, offered to let us live at his house; two foreigners with different customs. It's a little strange. They leave the house quite early, at 7.30am, and come back around 6pm. This means that we're alone in the house almost the whole day. They leave two strangers in their house. How mistaken many of us Argentinians are when we talk bad about or hate the English. Sadly I am, or was, one of them.

The Falklands War, in 1982, added to this historical rivalry between Argentinians and the English that can be perceived in political encounters, work meetings or in football matches. Sergio had always thought about this conflict.

How are they going to treat me being Argentinian? Will I have a disadvantage? Will they mention the war?

He predicted he would be treated differently because of his passport although there was no way to demonstrate it. The concept was more a fear than a reality – a "what *could* happen" not a "what *is* happening".

Chapter 2

Sergio had promised himself, after analysing it for a while, to make judgements based on first-hand experiences instead of basing them on ideas invented in his mind. He had always found answers through fictitious deduction and turned them into truths himself, even knowing there was room for mistakes. His life was full of various examples of this, some humorous and some startlingly deep. It's the same error that any human being would make not having exact evidence. The truth can be an entity that is easy to discover, but extremely difficult to prove. Unfortunately, most of us feel the necessity to give an opinion about everything or to always have an answer, even when the best or most sincere answer is: "I don't know."

Mum and dad
With the passing days, John, Mimi, Sergio and Cristian became like a little family with a daily routine. While the parents were at work, the boys took care of the chores. They kept the house neat and clean. Cristian cooked quite well and Paisa considered himself an exceptional kitchen helper, as he didn't even know how to boil pasta. He wanted to learn, but it was hopeless, and he left everything in the able hands of his 'brother'. For cultural reasons they rarely all sat down to eat together.

Sadly, there are few days we can eat dinner together. We've tried, but it doesn't work for us.

The Sergio Torres Story

It's tough to get used to eating so early. They eat dinner at 6.30pm, and us around 10pm. Normally, when they're having dinner, we have coffee and toast. Sometimes, if it ends up getting late on them, we all sit down together and we enjoy beautiful moments.

John speaks eight different languages. Yes, eight. He always speaks to us in Spanish because he wants the practice, but this is not very helpful for us.

Sometimes I get thinking and I can't believe that somebody can speak so many different languages. Our English is still pitiful and our Spanish isn't great either, as we still speak in our Mar del Plata slang. Luckily, Mimi is around. Even though she speaks French, English and Spanish, she wants us to learn English and always speaks to us in the local tongue. We are very grateful.

I love Argentina

For the next three months the boys lived comfortably in the warmth of a home, with their bellies full, only hungry for more football. Their performances received more praise daily and the high fives from their team-mates assured them that their play was being appreciated. Day by day, they improved on the pitch, playing with the style they liked playing with, without feeling pressure or having to think too much.

Chapter 2

Sergio was the most popular and considered one of the best players on the team. He played 20 matches that season, starting all of them, and scored four goals. Cristian played in 15 games (coming off the bench 11 times), scoring twice. Basingstoke's directors were extremely pleased with their play, especially with Paisa. It was not surprising then that at the end of the season they decided to renew the contracts for another year. Jorge Timoner managed the negotiations, securing them a raise. Perfect. It was time for Sergio to go back to Argentina, but on his terms: as a visitor, to relax and see his family, and later to return to Europe to continue following his dream.

There was something troubling him about going back. Seeing his family again would not be easy. On the flight to Buenos Aires he wondered how they would react to seeing him again, as his stay in England had extended longer than he had assured them at the beginning. He had told them he would be back in about three weeks and it had already been six months. In this time, he had learnt a million things and had had a life full of experiences.

The image of an imaginary world is always dissolved on encountering the real world, and this time would not be an exception. When Sergio found himself face to face with his family, he went directly to hug them, recharging his spent batteries and forgetting about his previous worries. His parents squeezed him so hard they almost hurt him. They wanted to touch him, kiss him, make sure he had been eating well.

During the emotional re-encounter, he realised he wasn't the same person as before. His arms were the same arms but the hugs felt different. He had left as Sergio Torres who had many doubts, and had returned as Sergio Torres, but with convictions. It was a different man coming back; probably not externally but he knew that inside something had changed. While he was in the UK, he had found the best school of learning, and now needed to rest and process everything that had happened to him.

During his visit to Argentina there was one special thing he needed to do – go to see his cousin's tomb – and he fulfilled this mission right away. He was respectfully mute while he was at the cemetery, once again feeling that silence was the best way to externalise his emotions. Later, he went to visit his uncle and family, still troubled by the decision he'd had to make after his cousin's death.

What do they think of me for not having come back immediately after?

He was relieved to find out that they had no hard feelings and that they also were staunch supporters of him fulfilling his dream, but at

Chapter 2

the same time sadness entered him, and it didn't take much for the tears to start falling when the memories began knocking on the door. They told him how the accident had happened. He tried to be strong and give them words of encouragement and strength, but his eyes betrayed him.

Working rules

Back in England, Sergio and Cristian found out that they wouldn't be paid during pre-season.

"What do you mean we don't get paid?!"

"It's always the same. These teams, during pre-season training, don't pay anybody. The salaries are only effective during the official season," Jorge Timoner tried to explain.

"But why?"

"Because Basingstoke is a semi-professional club, Sergio, not professional. You guys won't see a pound until the season starts. This is how it works, always."

"And how long does pre-season last?"

"Six weeks."

"Ugh!"

Pre-season was tough, with several friendly matches that helped to improve physical condition and touch. It was Sergio and Cristian's first pre-season in England and as they weren't 'professionals' they only practised on Tuesdays, Thursdays and Saturdays during this stage. The season started in the middle of August and, meanwhile, they needed to put their heads together and find a way to make some cash. Clearly, living with Mimi and John made things easier, but the boys didn't want to take advantage of their generosity any further. In other words, they needed to find work.

Mimi took them to a recruitment agency called Merit.

"Where are you taking us?"

"It's like an office that helps you find work."

Sergio and Cristian arrived confidently, they took a basic English test and passed it, even if just barely. "Thank God they stopped when they did!" thought Paisa. A week after the interview, they got a call and were given two positions at Boots, specialising in the buying and selling of products for hardware stores and pharmacies. They would be working in the warehouse from Monday to Friday, from 7am to 12noon.

> *It's just five hours, and afterwards we have plenty of time to train. Today we went to see the place and meet our supervisor. His name is Keith, and he seems pretty serious. He told us about the work and what we have to do, but we understood almost nothing, nodding our heads like always, so he wouldn't get upset. He could've even told us they were reducing our salary and we would've kept nodding our heads. It would suck if he found out on the first*

Chapter 2

day that we hardly know how to speak English. Keith gave us an all-blue uniform and later we went to buy some steel-toed boots, which are mandatory. Each one weighs four kilos and walking with so much weight for five hours is probably going to screw up our feet. Not good for a couple of football players, but tomorrow we'll see.

Be careful with that Argentinian

On their first day of work the boys were given carts and sent to work with Sandra, one of the most experienced employees. She explained to them what their tasks would be and how to do them. The job was easy and they didn't need to understand English perfectly to do it. On their carts they transported different types of products (shaving cream, razors, shampoo, etc) from the warehouse to the shelves. "This is a joke," they told each other.

After moving everything to its place, they had to open the boxes and bags, take everything out and separate it individually. That way, the clients could grab everything easier after making their order. As far as Sergio understood from Sandra, he had to work with the sponges and take them out of the bags, wearing the gloves he had been given.

When I had already opened a hundred packets, my hands started to feel wet. I looked at them and thought: 'I don't think this is supposed to happen.' It wasn't normal, so I went to find Sandra and show her. When she saw me, she yelled 'noooo!' 'Son of a bitch,' I thought. 'What a screw-up!' I understood her 'noooo!' perfectly. It wasn't necessary to translate. Sandra went to tell Keith and I realised that I had ruined the sponges because, evidently, they weren't meant to be opened. It wasn't so evident to me though and there was nothing we could do but throw them out. So, in my first four hours of work I had wasted £150, as each sponge cost £1.50. 'They're going to throw me out of here,' I thought, especially since I didn't think Keith was very friendly. Luckily, I escaped with only a yellow card.

The English clock

Sergio and Cristian were the youngest of the employees. Most of their workmates were between 40 and 60 years old. The age difference was a moot point because everybody had fun and acted like teenagers. Between work and training sessions with Basingstoke, the Argentinians woke up at six in the morning, ate toast and jam with coffee, and headed to work. John Gray had mentioned to the other club supporters that the two players were looking for a couple of used bicycles to get to work, in order to not spend their pay on the trip. In no time, one of the fans, called

Chapter 2

Lee, gave a bike of his to the boys to use, and they found a second for only £20.

At exactly noon, Sergio and Cristian finished their shift, got on their bikes and went home to take a nap before heading to practice, also with the bikes.

> *Our team-mates crack up laughing when they see us arrive on our bikes, especially when it rains, because we cover our shoes with rubbish bags to keep our feet dry. They all have nice cars, or at least 'normal' cars. We also laugh. Even the manager laughs. It's just that it's too far to walk and we don't want to take the bus, because it takes too long and costs too much. So we ride our bikes to all the practices and even on game day. They can't really complain. We arrive on time and have already warmed up.*

Once the season started, as they now had two incomes, Sergio and Cristian decided to move. They rented a cute, spacious house which they shared with Alex, a not-so-smiley South African. Meanwhile, at Boots, they soon became two of Keith's favourites, who, after the bad first impression, ended up being a kind and supportive person for them.

> *Keith loves football and we're playing for the local team – one of the reasons we have a bit*

The Sergio Torres Story

of an advantage. Sometimes I spend an hour or two talking to him about football. Despite my bad English, we understand each other. Sometimes I feel bad when my workmates walk by and I'm standing there, leaning against the shelves, chatting with him. But I'm not about to ignore my boss and say: 'Sorry, I have to work.' So I continue talking to him and I save myself more coming and going with those damn boots that weigh four kilos each.

Keith and John (a fellow employee) didn't miss a single match all season. Together, they were always the first to sit down in the stands and watch how Sergio and Cristian responded in every game, despite having accepted one hour more of work per day. Only three weeks after beginning with the company, they agreed to start their shift at six in the morning and still get off at noon.

The boys didn't want to entertain the possibility of a move to another club despite feeling that each week, with their constant improvement, they were surpassing the level of their club. Paisa preferred to continue creating his path by walking.

Hearts that walk
1 January was the first anniversary of Sergio Martín's death. That day, playing an away game against Maidenhead United, Paisa entered the pitch feeling a heavy emotional weight on his

Chapter 2

shoulders; not just because of his cousin, the primary cause, but also because his parents, his sister and his brother-in-law, Diego Verriello, were in the stands supporting him for the first time in England.

It was difficult for him to concentrate strictly on playing and not keep looking over to see the reactions of his loved ones. They had been saving for months for the trip to London, primarily so that Sergio didn't have to spend the holidays without the warmth of his family once again. Also in attendance was his friend Nicolás Uzquiano, who was playing in the Italian sixth division and who had come over to cheer him on. All five of them were staying at John and Mimi's house, something on which the couple had insisted, not a request of Sergio's.

> *They were the ones that wanted everyone to stay at their house. They went to France and left us the keys, surprising me once again. They're incredible.*

As always, actions speak louder than words and Mimi and John were perfect evidence. The couple demonstrated a clear difference between helping, a finite concept, and generosity, which has no limits. There are people willing to help in Europe, the Americas, Asia, Africa, Mars or Jupiter, spending their free time, giving money or resources, or sharing anything else extra available. However, generosity is sharing what you have, not what you don't need. It is not giving your neighbour your leftover bread from lunch, but instead inviting them to share the little you have at meal time. Mimi and John seemed to be giving free classes in understanding this concept. This was one truth for Sergio that was worth writing down in his diary.

That 1 January he was oozing with happiness at having such support in the stands and he wanted to thank them somehow, which he did. As if he had the power to create magic moments, he did nothing more than score the opening goal, and in doing so caused ecstasy among his five closest fans. Probably, for the first time ever in this category, you could hear "gooooooal!" louder than "yeeeeeeees!"

> Cristian dealt me an incredible assist, unselfishly, as he was one on one with the keeper, but he passed it to me, as if he was saying: 'You need this.'

The goal dedication was obvious. Almost instinctively, after seeing the ball in the back of the net, Sergio's legs seemed to move by themselves towards where his family was seated, while he looked up at them, pointing. For Sergio, this moment was comparable to the satisfaction

Chapter 2

of winning a title. The match finished 1-1; an unimportant detail.

Asleep on the job

> Today Keith told us that he'd had a meeting with his bosses and that they have to change the work schedule. All the employees have to work two Saturdays a month. Cristian and I don't know what to do, as we have matches on Saturdays. Keith even tried speaking with the bosses specifically about us, but they told him there were no exceptions. We have to agree or quit.

Sergio and Cristian were not prepared to leave the club after all they had been through, but they didn't want to lose their jobs either because they needed the money. Keith, understanding perfectly the situation, fixed things so they could work the Saturdays that Basingstoke had home games, as it would be impossible to work on days with away matches because of the travelling. This way they could fulfil both commitments, even if they would be a little tired during the matches.

The first Saturday that they had to double up happened to be the day of the game against Grays Athletic, the current league leaders. That day, they got up at 5am, had breakfast and got on their bikes at 5.30am to head to work. They worked from 6am to 12noon and after, got back on their bikes and arrived home at 12.30pm. They had a shower, ate some pasta and left the house again with the bikes at 1.15pm to ride the 15 minutes to the stadium, where they had to be at 1.30pm. They didn't even have time to take a nap. One of the consequences came to light immediately. In the locker room, while the manager was giving his pre-game speech, Sergio's eyes began to close.

I fell asleep, but probably just for a few seconds, I guess. I don't know. As I didn't understand anything the manager was saying, added to being tired, I couldn't help it. Cristian, who was next to me, elbowed me and woke me up. Luckily, I don't think anybody noticed, because if they had, they would've kicked me out or fined me. When I woke up, I did what I could to pretend nothing had happened and kept my eyes open, pretty much using my hands and pretending there was something in my eye. But in the end, the match didn't go so badly. I was named man of the match.

Strengthening the clan

A new Argentinian joined Basingstoke at the beginning of 2005. His name was Germán de la Vega, a winger with exceptional technique, who immediately integrated himself into the group without formalities. Sergio and Cristian already knew him as Jorge Timoner had introduced them

Chapter 2

all the previous July, but he hadn't been able to stay for administrative reasons. As he didn't have money or a place to stay, Paisa invited him to stay at the house he was renting with Cristian and Alex, the South African. In spite of not having much room for him, Sergio applied what he had learnt from Mimi and John. After receiving so much, a desire to give had arisen in him.

> *We have three small rooms in the house. One is Alex's, which we can't touch, as we don't have a good relationship with him. In another room, which is a little bigger, Cristian stays with his girlfriend, Laura. I live in the other, much smaller one. So, I told Germán he could stay in my room. We put a mattress on the floor and now there's barely room to walk. But the good thing about all of this is that when we go to work, he stays home and has lunch ready when we get back.*

Sergio and Germán began to form a close friendship quickly. They had met each other a short time before but they behaved like two boys who had gone to school together their whole lives. About the same time, Cristian, who had never been a big fan of going out at night anyway, stopped going out to the pubs with Paisa and started spending more time with Laura, his girlfriend, who had moved from Argentina to live with him.

The Sergio Torres Story

I used to get really bored. I wanted to go out at night, but didn't have anyone to go with. But now, with Germán here, it's different. We go out on Wednesdays and Saturdays. Even though we don't have much money, we have a good time, but it's not like you really need much money to have fun.

Rich or poor were two terms for him that had nothing to do with finances. Sergio believed that he could be happy just satisfying his basic needs, although sometimes it was difficult for him to define exactly what these needs were. He no longer believed in the ever popular rule which says "you are what you have". He was sure he could be comfortable in other ways and that he could be rich in what he thought was important. He believed himself to be strong enough to ignore the obligation to consume the things our consumer society imposes.

Germán and I have fun, with or without money. We still go to the bars in the centre but we do it in our own way. It's really cold here these days. We take the bikes and start riding towards the centre. It's about 20 minutes. We wear our long coats and bring a nylon bag along. Two minutes before arriving, there are some bushes. We take off the coats, we put them in the nylon bags and we hide them. We get to the centre, where all the

Chapter 2

girls with short skirts and high heels are, and pass quickly with the bikes so nobody sees our faces. Then we park the bikes really close and lock them up in ten seconds. We show up, acting cool as if we just got out of the car.

The South American mansion

At this point, Sergio wasn't as affected by negative circumstances as he was before. He wouldn't even use the word "dramatic" to define them. Things hurt less when you're used to the pain. It is like fighting with Mike Tyson in the preliminary rounds, and then taking blows from a weak teenager. That was why, after their six-month contract ran out on the house and the owner didn't want to renew their contract, Paisa wasn't too alarmed. He was above worrying. He just needed to deal with the situation. He tried to change the owner's mind but he couldn't convince him.

The two boys had had a few arguments with him when they believed the place needed repairs and, furthermore, Alex, the South African, was not very pleased that Germán had been invited to live there by Sergio and wasn't paying a thing (not that he had anything, of course). Laura, Cristian's girlfriend, had gone back to Argentina and it was the same story as before: once again, in England, three Argentinians with no home and no place to go.

The Sergio Torres Story

When you walk through a storm
Hold your head up high
And don't be afraid of the dark
At the end of the storm
Is a golden sky
And the sweet silver song of a lark
Walk on through the wind
Walk on through the rain
Though your dreams be tossed and blown
Walk on, walk on, with hope in your heart
And you'll never walk alone
You'll never walk alone
Walk on, walk on, with hope in your heart
And you'll never walk alone
You'll never walk alone

Liverpool FC anthem

The most obvious option was to return to Mimi and John's house, but they considered this an abuse of their kindness, so they decided to speak with the club manager about the problem and try to find a solution. They had nothing to lose, but what they didn't expect was the odd remedy he would propose to them. Ernie Howe offered to let them sleep in a room under the stands, next to the visitors' locker room, where the club directors and owners got together to have coffee and eat delicacies on game days.

We sleep in the room they call the 'boardroom'. It's pretty nice, is carpeted and has two bath-

Chapter 2

rooms: men and women. The manager and his assistant got us two beds that you can fold in half easily. They also brought us a separate mattress because one of us has to sleep on the floor. I volunteered because it doesn't bother me. I actually think I like it. They also gave us a camping stove with gas, so we can cook and eat here. We also have a sink and a tap, and even a TV. We've got it all.

The only problem is that on game days we have to pick everything up, even the beds, and store it all behind one of the walls where there's space to hide everything. We also have to clean and vacuum the carpet.

After the first month of living underneath the stands, the three Argentinians started to see the glass half full with optimism. Although in the back of their heads they were a little worried, they decided to take advantage of their favourable situation, described by Sergio in his diary:

We talked about the positive aspects and we realised there are a bunch of them. First and foremost is that we don't have to ride our bikes to practice sessions or matches. Furthermore, since we've been staying here, we haven't been late to practice once. We are also much closer to the centre and we don't have to take the bikes when we go out at night. As if this wasn't enough, many afternoons we take advantage of our time and we go to the 'park' next to our 'house', the football pitch, to kick the ball around and simulate plays. But the icing on the cake is that Keith, our supervisor at Boots, lives close to here and sometimes comes to pick us up for work and later, brings us home, saving us the freezing bike ride.

Basingstoke had a very good season. It was considered a big success by some of the happiest people who had fresh in their minds the weak and insufficient performances of the year before. Everybody, both optimists and pessimists, gave the thumbs-up. The team finished in sixth place, almost making the play-offs. League rules stated that the first-placed team were promoted automatically, and the second- to fifth-placed teams had a play-off to decide which other team would join them.

Sergio finished the league better than had been expected from the beginning. He was the star of the team, hero of the young and the old, and the fans had fallen in love with this skilled and hard-working kid from the countryside. His statistics justified their opinion of him; he started all 46 matches of the season and scored four goals.

His friends weren't far behind him: Cristian played 35 games, coming off the bench eight times, and scored 13 goals, including one hat-

Chapter 2

trick, while Germán de la Vega started 17 matches, a significant figure taking into account that he signed with the club during the second half of the season.

Together again

Perhaps it's because the earth is round or perhaps it's just a silly belief, but sometimes, to get closer to someone, you have to distance yourself. The thousands of miles and the enormous Atlantic Ocean standing between Great Britain and Mar del Plata ended up being the reason that stronger ties were created between Sergio and his family. Their separation united them. The distance, although at times saddening, brought out a previously unknown necessity and strengthened the existing love.

During that off-season, after their impressive play with Basingstoke, the trio separated for two months. Cristian had decided to travel to Spain to visit some family there. Germán, without many options, stayed in England. Paisa had told his parents that this year he wouldn't go to Argentina because, he told them, he wanted to take advantage of his time in the UK to visit other European cities. His mother didn't like the idea but tried to hide her disappointment.

I think they're pretty bummed out, but they believed it. A surprise is in the making. The only

> *people who know I'm going to Mar del Plata are Germán, Cristian, John and Mimi, but they can't say anything. I've told them to keep their mouths shut.*

During the flight to Buenos Aires, Sergio speculated how his family would react to seeing him suddenly in the city of the sea, the waves and the wind. What will they think? How will they feel? How will they act? Because he spent so much time analysing the situation, the trip seemed shorter than normal. Once again, just like the year before, he felt like a different person returning to Argentina. A different Paisa. There was only one thing in his soul that hadn't changed in almost two years of being away: his utopia of being a professional footballer.

At eight o'clock in the morning, on a Saturday, he showed up at home with his bags. He rang the bell without knowing if anyone was home or if they were all sleeping. At the beginning, there was no answer. He knocked loudly on the door and kept knocking until his mother stuck her head out of the window. At first, she didn't recognise who it was, but then she saw the big, blonde curls.

"Sergio! What are you doing here?! Did they kick you out?" his mum Mabel exclaimed, pale and frightened.

She was alone at home and was so upset that her hands were shaking as she opened the door.

Chapter 2

"Relax mum. Nothing's wrong. Open the door and I'll explain. Everything's fine. They didn't kick me out."

His sister, Rosana, would be the next surprised person. She was studying at a school in the centre of Mar del Plata, where she was taking a computer course. Sergio, who had gone to pick her up, hid quietly behind a plant and, when he saw her leave the building with a friend, he jumped out suddenly. Her reaction came from deep down in her heart; she began to cry right there. Her classmate was frozen there watching them give each other what seemed an eternal hug.

Only one last hug remained to be shared; with his father, Raúl, who had taken Rosana's boyfriend, Diego Verriello, to Olavarría, a city near Mar del Plata, where he had a car race. Raúl was the co-driver and he also enjoyed keeping the vehicle maintained. Paisa went to the race wearing a hood so he wouldn't recognise him, entered the garage and sat down behind the wheel of the car while his father was talking with the crew. In this moment, being in on the surprise, they told his father: "Raúl, Raúl! Get going! We have to start!"

Raúl, who hadn't thought it was time yet, did what they said and headed towards the car adjusting his jump suit.

"Let's go Raúl! Move it!" exclaimed Sergio from inside the car.

Raúl nodded his head but then spotted Diego, the driver, outside the car still.

"What's going on here?! Who's inside the car, then?!"

Paisa stuck his head out the window and caught his father's eyes.

Later, Raúl told the story: "He was wearing a helmet, so I didn't recognise him, but when I saw his eyes inside the helmet, I almost died. I forgot everything. I just wanted to squeeze him." At first he reacted like his wife, almost having a heart attack, and after, hugged him like you hug someone that you never want to escape. Sergio wrote about it in his diary (already his second notebook):

> *The reunion with my loved ones was phenomenal and the surprise was beautiful. Difficult to explain. Their first reactions scared me quite a bit, especially my mum's. I think now, that something could've happened to her. She was extremely startled. I'll never do that again. Never.*

When a friend says goodbye

Midway through 2005, Sergio went back to England to continue building the path that would lead him to his dream. He had already been on British soil for two years but still hadn't become the professional footballer that he so much

Chapter 2

desired to be. He tried, he worked, he fell down, he got back up and he kept dreaming more and more. Surprisingly, he kept his head held high but continued wondering how long he would have to wait. He wanted to live off football and was convinced he would be able to, but the months went rapidly and life accelerated, passing by quickly.

He knew he was already 24. Sometimes his subconscious asked him if he had already wasted too much time. Every once in a while, he also became consumed by the annoying critiques that he had heard at the beginning, claiming he was mad and acting foolishly, and didn't recognise the courage he had had up to this point to do what his critics would never be brave enough to do because of the possible consequences or what people could say.

The script of his film had been modified many times, but he had already assumed the risk, taking comfort in an old adage: however painful the journey might be, the most painful thing of all would have been to never set off. He remained convinced and told himself he would stand tall as long as his dreams were alive, and this was a reassurance because he knew that nobody, even in their wildest dreams, could take his away.

For the next season, Sergio would return to Basingstoke, who were looking to move up to the fifth tier of English football. He was expecting a complicated year as he would no longer be sharing his life in Great Britain with his team-mate, flatmate and friend, through good times and bad, Cristian Levis. There were going separate ways after a year and a half of living together.

"Goodbyes are such sweet pain." (*Gualicho, Patricio Rey y sus Redonditos de Ricota*)

Cristian had met a Spanish girl and love was obligating him to pack his bags and move to Spain. With one decision, Cristian was losing everything he had slowly and painfully won. He was leaving the club with which he competed in the English sixth division and he would be missing, after all his hard work, the possible ascent to a higher league. He was leaving his job, his English friends, Paisa, Germán and a possible future in Great Britain. Sergio was not convinced that he had the right to try to talk him out of his decision, as he too had listened to his heart and made sacrifices to do the mad things it had told him.

This would not be the only separation Paisa would have to deal with during that time. The other, however, was his choice: the agent-player relationship he had with Jorge Timoner had run out.

We were having a few problems. There are some things I don't like about him; the way he does certain things. That's why I think it's better to end our professional relationship. I feel bad about it because Jorge has helped me a lot and,

Chapter 2

thanks to him, I'm still playing in England, but I think that this separation will be for the best; referring to work-related stuff. But I will always be incredibly thankful for what he has done for me and, luckily, we will remain friends.

Back and to the right
The fact that the world is full of contradictions is nothing new for Sergio. When he was back at home, he used to count the hours until it was time to go train, and then when he was training, he sometimes counted the minutes until he could go home to rest. When he was in England, he waited eagerly for his holiday time so he could go back and see his family, and when he was with his family, he waited anxiously to head back to Europe with the hope of, once and for all, fulfilling his dream. He was living the future instead of the present, which at times, worried him.

Returning, once again, also meant going back to work at Boots, where he was very comfortable despite the complication it presented, especially on the days of home games.

The days when I work in the morning, and later have a match, are incredibly hard. I end up destroyed.

Germán de la Vega and Sergio continued living together but, in this new stage, once again, they had to pack up their belongings and move. It wasn't right to keep living in the 'boardroom' in Basingstoke's stadium. Where would they go? They ended up back in Mimi and John's house again; a place Sergio had left before, not wanting to take advantage of the couple's generosity.

The art of dreaming
In a friendly match at the beginning of pre-season, Basingstoke faced Wycombe Wanderers, a professional team from the fourth division. Sergio was placed on the pitch as an attacking midfielder, giving him more freedom. They also asked him to guard the opposing team's star, Rob Lee, who had played previously for Newcastle and who had also been a part of the English national team during the 1998 World Cup in France. "Nice challenge," he thought.

Paisa stepped up to the challenge convinced of his ability. How couldn't he? He is the one that had wanted to go to the dance and now that the music was playing, he couldn't change his mind. He took a deep breath, put his head up, clenched his teeth and, in the end, stood out above the rest of his team-mates.

As the result showed, his grand performance didn't serve for much (Basingstoke lost 7-2) and his good play was overshadowed by the team's lack of success. However, the next day, he got a surprise. John Gorman, the manager

Chapter 2

of Wycombe, had been impressed with the Argentinian's display and had spoken with Ernie Howe about wanting to see Sergio in action again, but this time playing for Wycombe in a friendly match against Stevenage the following day.

> *This is my big opportunity to sign with a professional club. Once again I'll have the chance to show what I can do. If this game goes well, I'll be able to try out with this team and have the possibility of signing my first professional contract.*

At the beginning, he didn't know how to react when Ernie Howe gave him the news. Sergio told him that he was "dead", that he couldn't move because he had run so much the previous day, that he was out of shape having recently returned from his holidays and that he wouldn't be able to perform as well as he wanted because there weren't even 48 hours to recover between the matches.

"OK, Sergio. If you don't feel right, I'll tell him you aren't going and that you're going to keep playing with us. I'll be happy because I don't want to lose you," his manager told him.

"No, please. Don't say anything. I'll go play the game tomorrow."

He couldn't let the opportunity pass him by. The betting table was open and he had to put money down. There had to be a place to make his dreams become real, and this place might be Wycombe. In order to be sure, he had to go there. He knew that it would be difficult to respond physically but that it would be even more painful to not show up than to be rejected.

> *I don't want to get too excited. I called my family to tell them the news and they were super happy. I told them it was just a trial and that there was nothing for sure, something I know from experience. What I was told, after being turned down in Brighton almost two years ago, still hurts: 'He's a good player, but he doesn't have the speed or the strength to play football in England.' My dad told me to play relaxed and to do what I know, nothing different, but it's difficult to control my nerves. I'm trying, but it's hard.*

Sergio then called Keith to ask for the day off, explaining the situation and the importance of the match. Keith, already conscious of Sergio's dream (they had spoken about it many times), not only gave him permission, but enthusiastically wished him "good, good luck". In a car together with Ernie Howe, Pete Peters and Germán, Sergio Torres was on his way to his big test, knowing it was one of those days, one of those moments, in which he had to give it his all.

Chapter 2

I couldn't move my legs. I was extremely tired and very nervous.

They entered the training ground. It was Bisham Abbey, where England's national team had practised years before.

There was something like an old castle there and amazing pitches with pristine grass. Shockingly, it is only used for friendlies.

John Gorman greeted him and very politely accompanied him to the locker room where the team was.

I was embarrassed, but the guys remembered me from the match we had played two days before, and they welcomed me saying I was a good player.

Paisa put on his boots, they handed him his shirt and Wycombe's manager told him he would be playing the first and last 30 minutes: the game was divided into three equal periods. During the first 30 minutes, Sergio stood out strongly. He won balls, and didn't lose them, he passed well, at times controlling the midfield, co-ordinating attacks and managing the defence, doing exactly what he needed to do at all the right times.

The Sergio Torres Story

> *At the end of the first period I went over to Ernie, Pete and Germán excitedly. 'If I continue playing this way, they'll keep me,' I thought. 'They're going to let me try out.'*

However, the last 30 minutes were a disaster for the Argentinian, and what had been a sunny morning turned into an afternoon with dark clouds announcing a storm.

> *My muscles had got cold and my legs weighed about 20 kilos each. Nothing went right, not even one good pass. I couldn't have played worse, even if they'd asked me. I was incredibly upset with myself.*

Reasoning told him that once again he had lost the opportunity to be a professional football player and that his trial with Wycombe was over. Another train lost.

> *What an idiot!*

The verdict

John Gorman created no illusions when he said goodbye to Sergio, who then assumed that he wouldn't be taking part in the trial. He had his head hung low until Ernie Howe appeared. He had been speaking to Wycombe's manager.

Chapter 2

"He is very happy with how you played the first 30 minutes, but can't understand why you played so bad in the last 30."

"I know. I'm out of the trial."

"I explained that your fitness isn't very good and that you've just come back from holiday."

"OK, thanks. But it doesn't matter now."

"He decided to give you a trial. He wants to watch your performance for the next few days and then decide if you'll be part of the team for the season."

A rainbow appeared in his sky. After two years, his chance had come back around. Once again, Sergio had the possibility of becoming a professional footballer. He would have a trial with fourth division Wycombe. Another door to his fantasy had opened for him. The utopia was looking more and more real, and his dream was turning to reality.

Chapter 3

"Those who walk know that every step counts, but the path only becomes clear upon arriving at the destination."
      Sub-commander Marcos

ANOTHER TRIAL, another challenge. The latest grand challenge for Sergio was to control his body among such intense agitation. How would he handle the trial weeks with Wycombe? In other words, how would he face his ghosts with a level head? In this context, asking his legs not to shake and his mind to think clearly would have been like climbing Mount Aconcagua, the highest mountain in the southern hemisphere. If he could conquer his fears, it would be much easier to resist the pressure, keeping in mind, however, that without fears, we aren't really human beings.

For Sergio, it didn't seem like a good idea to lose contact with his emotions, at least on the unsure journey he was on. Every three steps he

Chapter 3

took while paying attention to his heart, he took one tremulous step back while listening to reason. His flawed nature determined his pace and didn't allow him to advance any other way.

He got shivers just thinking about signing with a professional club. Deep down inside he was smiling because he realised that this was what he really wanted and what he had been searching for since he could remember, but at the same time he was experiencing inevitable panic. Fears, reminding him of past failures, came back to life. He had thought about it and desired it for so long that being so close to finally living his dream caused him to be uneasy and tense. There was no simple way to control himself. He wanted to ignore this fear that would impair his performance, or throw it to the ground and stomp on it a thousand times. He wanted to relax and simply perform, disregard his apprehension, but it wasn't that easy.

One conflict in particular bothered him. On the pitch he felt confident and strong, but away from the field he lost his strength and was consumed by worries. He was engaged in hand to hand combat with his mind and the bell to end the round wouldn't ring. If a doubt came to his mind, immediately 20 more would appear. His childhood fears arrived along with his teenage preoccupations and his shyness continued to haunt him. His off-the-pitch ruminations were inconclusive. He decided to take this present struggle like any other that appears during our lives and apply a strategy against the battles in his mind that, many times seeming eternal, are usually the most dangerous and disloyal to the individual. He would use the following method: recognise his points of tension, figure out where they were coming from, learn to live with them and later overcome them.

The last turn

Sergio spoke immediately with Keith about getting two days off of work per week so he could practise with Wycombe.

"Take off whichever days you need. This is your dream. Your chance is now," answered his supervisor.

Keith's "now" seemed to echo when he said it. Why now? Why not before? Why can't it be later?

Paisa began to prepare himself for the trial mentally and physically. High Wycombe was quite far from Basingstoke and there were no direct trains. He would have to first take a train to London and, from there, catch another to the training ground. It would be two hours' travelling time in total.

It'll be tough, but I can't complain. This is what I want.

Chapter 3

John Gorman talked to Ernie Howe and mentioned that it just so happened there was a girl who worked in Wycombe's offices and lived in Basingstoke, and she drove to the club every morning. The drive was barely an hour. When he heard the welcome news, Sergio immediately called the girl, Sarah. Under these circumstances, he couldn't be too shy to ask for favours.

> *Without asking any questions, she said 'yes' immediately. She explained, as if it would be a problem for me, that she would be picking me up very early. We've started making the trip together twice a week. My English still isn't too good, so speaking with her on the drive is really helping me to improve.*

Stefan Oakes and Clint Easton were the first two players from Wycombe to approach Sergio on the first day, help him out and make sure he was alright. The ice was breaking quickly. There was no need to wait for it to melt.

> *They're funny guys. They both talk to me really quickly and I understand about half of what they say, but they still make me laugh a lot.*

Sergio was working at Boots and involved in preseason with Basingstoke preparing for their new campaign in English football's sixth tier, and was attending practices twice a week with Wycombe, trying to take the step up to the fourth division and professional football. This would be enough to make one dizzy, or to fly, although he still had his feet on the ground.

Paisa had always had the peculiarity of seeing the universe through a keyhole, focusing on or emphasising the simple things and ignoring the luxurious; things that the majority of people focus their attention on. This way of looking at the world would inevitably change during this time. Things he saw and experienced while training with a professional club seduced him: the training pitches had amazing grass, the pleasant locker rooms, the impressively equipped gym and the attentive people that constantly helped him. He was seeing the other faces of the world and felt the need to get to know them well.

> *It's like a different world, an incredible life. Luxurious. Something is always surprising me. I'm like a kid observing everything and enjoying it all, as if it were a new toy. I find myself saying 'wow!' at times. After every practice, we head for the impressive stadium, where we eat together. I'm doing everything I can to be able to stay here.*

Something new came to light. He seemed to find another dream which he had never considered

Chapter 3

before. His desire had been to play professional football, nothing more, but now he was also fantasising about the magic and the little extras that existed in this new world. Naturally, he was being seduced.

The Theatre of Dreams
Meanwhile, at Basingstoke, Paisa was the most pampered player on the team and the favourite of all the directors. He was also getting gifts, attention and other accolades from the fans. Before the end of the previous season they had made him a new offer: he would become the best paid player of the squad, making £500 per week. His contract had a special clause as well. If any team from a higher level was interested in him, he would be allowed to negotiate with them.

Although he was comfortable, loved and very happy there, it wasn't what he wanted, and furthermore he only practised twice a week, in the evenings, and had to maintain a job to get by.

Among all the different gifts he was receiving, one was extra special. Steve Murfitt, one of the club directors, invited him to go see Manchester United play against Newcastle. When he heard the offer, Sergio got big eyes as he still hadn't been to a Premier League stadium to see a match. This was due to the fact that the ticket price, added to the train fare, was too much money for him. As destiny would have it, his first time would be at Old Trafford, the celebrated Theatre of Dreams.

When I entered, I was blown away. I froze. Seeing such a stadium and so many people paralysed me. There were 75,000 people there. It turned out that our seats were right behind where Rooney scored an incredible goal. He's a monster. He was arguing with the referee but play continued, he took off running and a bad clearance came to his feet outside the box. He drilled it with his first touch into the top corner. This guy is unbelievable. It would be amazing to play there one day.

He shared every one of these sensations with his family, his great support from the fields of Mar del Plata.

"The stadium is enormous, dad. Impressive. It's all fantastic. It would be a dream to play there one day. Do you think I could?"

"Why not 'Borromeo'? You have a better chance than me." Raúl Torres delicately sidestepped the question.

Paisa was an eternal optimist. He dreamed big but lived small.

The final stretch

It wasn't Sergio's first trial on English soil. He had done the same with Brighton (rejected after

Chapter 3

two weeks), with Woking (he had to abandon the trial after arguing with Roland), with Molesey (accepted after one day) and with Basingstoke (accepted after half a practice as he arrived late). Now, this time, the physical, tactical and technical tests seemed never-ending. He had been practising with Wycombe twice a week for almost a month, but he still didn't know if he would end up on the team. He was getting more agitated every day and once again, the words "failure", "disillusion" and "rejection" came to mind, perhaps because he was trying with all his might to forget them.

As if all this on his mind wasn't enough, in August Basingstoke's season would be starting and Sergio would have to play in their colours (wearing number seven or eight) while he awaited Wycombe's decision. His troubled mind was pressured even further.

The fans, while awaiting the decision, had a curious way of expressing themselves. They knew the Argentinian wanted to become a full-time professional, that at the time he was trying out with another team and that they could possibly be losing him soon. However, at the beginning of the season, they cheered him on even stronger than before, while at the same time desiring that he would reach his goal. As before, the small club was making a meaningful gesture. They were putting people before results.

The Sergio Torres Story

During this complicated time for Sergio, Mimi and John continued their untiring support for him. The house was more and more delightful for him every day. John was his number one fan and had an amazing memory. He remembered all of Sergio's matches to the last detail: how many shots on target he had, how many minutes he had played and the fouls he had committed.

In the first three matches of the season, Paisa demonstrated his superior talent with the ball, much to the satisfaction of his fans, and further strengthening his confidence. Although not known as a goalscorer but rather as a ball controller and playmaker, he scored two goals during the three games.

"Training with us is making you a better player," John Gorman congratulated him, with his smiling but mysterious face. The manager of Wycombe Wanderers seemed to be hiding something behind his moustache. It was difficult to know what it was during those days of tension and the two of them weren't on close enough terms yet for Sergio to ask. At this point, Gorman preferred to avoid the subject of the contract.

I really don't know if he wants me or not. If he wanted me, I should have already signed.

The transfer window was closing at the end of August. Until then, there was time to hear good

Chapter 3

news or bad news. It had already been 30 days since the trial had started.

The days he didn't go to Wycombe, Sergio had to work from 6am until noon. He was already missing a lot of work and this was not good. Luckily Keith, who had become a friend and many times travelled more than an hour to watch his games, continued giving him permission to miss work whenever necessary.

The chequered flag

Many times, what you had been hoping would come knocking on your door seems to arrive after you've already put on your robe and slippers. There were no exceptions in this story. The most desired decision would fall from the sky when least expected; minutes before Basingstoke would visit Eastbourne.

Ernie Howe took Sergio aside to talk with him in private: "Today is going to be your last game with us. I've spoken with John Gorman and he told me he wants you to sign this week."

"..."

"Sergio, I want you to play fearlessly today. I want you to finish strong and help us win."

Once again the tide had turned and Sergio found himself on the crest of the wave. The moment he had waited so long for had finally arrived.

It made me very happy when Ernie told me the news. I felt true happiness for the first time. Later, we won the match 3-2. It was my last with Basingstoke. It was a shame it couldn't have been in front of the home fans, but I'm very happy anyway. I'm going to make a living playing football. It took me almost two years but I've done it. I'll be doing what I love, what I've always wanted to do.

This story of a passionate search would have a happy ending. The twee saying "dreams really can become reality" was worth believing. Paisa could proudly raise the cup because he never gave up.

Love in the time of cholera
In this world, there are talkers and there are doers, and each individual chooses for themselves who they will be. Sergio Torres, who had declared war on formality, was destroying the labels people had stuck on him. His love for football, a true feeling that came from deep down inside him, was overcoming everyone's negativity. He still hadn't crossed the finish line, but every step had been meaningful and had taught him valuable lessons.

In Argentina, he would have always been preoccupied with work, money, the future and what people say, but in England, he learnt that when he stopped thinking about all these things, he was at peace. The love that had forced him to

Chapter 3

exchange comfort for insecurity also gave him the strength to face anything. He had made the leap when he chose to abandon security and conformity to search for a happiness that was difficult to find. Perseverance had come along on the trip and had helped him on the path, picking him up and setting him on his feet each time he had fallen. It had been a long journey and only the last step remained, but the time had come.

Ernie Howe called him on 24 August to tell him that the next day he would be taking him to his first official training with Wycombe. He was parading past the chequered flag and was close to the victory lane. He was 24 years old.

Diary. 25 August 2005

After practice, the three of us got together: Ernie, John and I. Wycombe's manager told me he wanted to give me a two-year contract. The money is not the best since they're not sure how I'll perform at this level. At the beginning, I'll be making about the same as I'm making with Basingstoke, but there's a re-negotiation clause after 20 games. I don't mind right now. I'm going to be a professional footballer! After almost two years of living in England, I'm going to live my dream.

The Sergio Torres Story

Ernie Howe helped him with the contract negotiation as Sergio wasn't sure about some of the terms. However, the numbers and the jargon didn't figure in his notebook, where he would be crossing out the bold print that said "account pending". A calculator, which so accurately handles figures, would never be able to measure his satisfaction, as the most valuable treasures are not kept in banks, nor can you count them.

I think I had to sign about 25 different pieces of paper. This is incredible.

After signing his first professional contract and being interviewed twice (first for a newspaper and second for the club), Sergio called his family to give them the good news. Having somebody to share his happiness with made it all the more significant to him.

Dream fulfilled

Sergio a few days after arriving in Great Britain, here posing with Roland's car.

Alongside his friendly Cameroonian house-mate in his first house.

Sergio and Pablo – plus their inseparable football – outside the Hilton Hotel in Paddington.

With Cristian Levis a few days after the pair were re-united.

Sergio's first visit to Buckingham Palace – but not his last.

Mimi and John gave Sergio a home when one was most required.

The family – John, Sergio, Mimi and Cristian.

Cristian, Sergio and German playing for Basingstoke Town.

The boys while on a break together.

Sergio on his first visit to Old Trafford, when he wondered if he would one day play there.

The Wycombe Wanderers club shop sold a range of Sergio Torres wigs in honour of the fan favourite (thanks to Paul Dennis and Wycombe Wanderers for the picture).

Sergio's father, Raúl wears a wig in support of his son.

The Torres family – mother Mabel, father Raúl and sister Rosana on a visit to see Sergio play.

Little sister. Here Sergio is with Claire, daughter of Tom and Elaine in his first house in Wycombe.

At the second attempt, Sergio gets his picture with Frank Lampard.

Sergio, on the day he borrowed clothes so he could go in the box at Stamford Bridge, alongside Jorge Timoner.

Sergio challenges Andriy Shevchenko in front of 42,000 people at Stamford Bridge.

Sergio shows off his shirt after signing for Peterborough United, his fourth English club (thanks to Terry Harris for the picture).

Chasing his idol Carlos Tevez in a game against Manchester United.

Tevez and Torres ... the former Boca Juniors hero signed autographs for Sergio and his father.

Celebrating promotion to the Championship with his two best friends, Russell Martin and Chris Whelpdale, and team physio Keith Oakes.

Sergio takes on Fabricio Coloccini, his fellow countryman, for Peterborough against Newcastle.

Flanked by Coloccini and Jonas Gutierrez, another Argentine, after the match.

All smiles after signing on loan for Lincoln City (thanks to Lincoln City for the picture).

Sergio dances through the rain in the FA Cup tie against Derby County.

Going crazy after scoring the winner in the last minute against the Rams.

Paisa 1 Rooney 0 – the Argentine pushes past the England striker and comes away with the ball.

Clapping the supporters with pride after giving everything at Old Trafford.

A cherished memory from a picture with Rooney after the game.

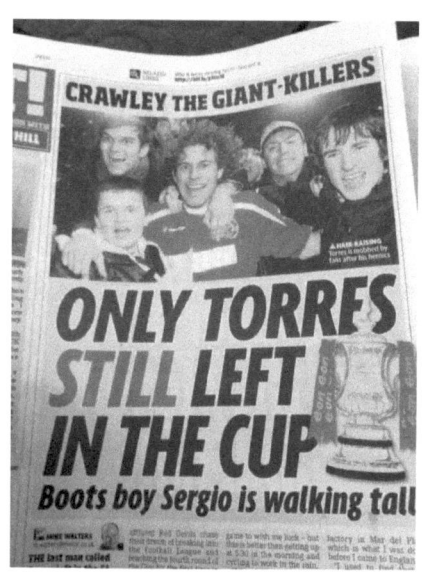

Newspaper coverage of the run to the fifth round of the FA Cup.

A perfect day for a wedding.

The Torres family – Sergio, wife Lena and daughter Luna.

Sergio and Juan Manuel López, the writers of The Sergio Torres Story, *at the Emirates Stadium to see Arsenal vs Everton.*

Chapter 4

"After climbing a great hill, one only finds that there are many more hills to climb."
Nelson Mandela

AND NOW, God? And now that the dream has been fulfilled? What path should I take? What tools should I use and where do I get the motivation? Why should I continue? What exists beyond great dreams? How can all the strength gained during the last two years be put to use? Should I get rid of them or hold on to them? And what about the lessons learnt? And what about the coming melancholy? Do I lose the ability to dream and the purpose to continue climbing? Where should I stop? Where is the top? What do I do at the end of the page? Write another paragraph? Why? Do I need another lifetime to get even further or should I just enjoy the conquest? Do I just plant the flag and stop advancing? Does time stop? Does the battery of the imagination ever run out? How many utopias can one man create? New doors to new dreams are waiting ...

Turning the page

English professional football is divided into four divisions: Premier League (first division), Championship (second division), League 1 (third division) and League 2 (fourth division, in which Wycombe were competing).

Having a professional contract obligated Sergio Torres to dedicate himself 100 per cent to his new club, but first he needed to take care of something important: to go and say goodbye to his workmates at Boots. He had worked for a year at the distributing company and had many fond memories, things he would remember as treasures, later to be told as stories; the kind of stories which allow us to feel alive.

On his last day of work there were many kind words and meaningful gestures. Even though goodbyes can be painful, everybody was happy that the Argentinian would finally be living his dream.

It had seemed an unreachable objective and had become a goal for all, so the whole group was sharing in the happiness. There was sadness in the goodbyes and many times sadness causes one to meditate, meditation can lead to melancholy, and melancholy can turn even the simplest man into a poet.

Chapter 4

Sergio thanked them heartily for the time they had spent together. All of his workmates together wished him luck on writing a new page of his life. Old Keith was genuine. He would even start driving the 90 minutes to go watch Paisa's home games. Words were not needed to express the feelings that had grown between them.

As for Germán de la Vega, he also would be packing his bags to leave Basingstoke Town. He had decided, before Sergio had even signed his contract with Wycombe, to go back to Argentina because of passport problems.

Getting accustomed

After the signing and the welcoming formalities, Sergio was on the squad list for Wycombe's first league match at Shrewsbury. He would be staying with the team in a classy hotel and was impressed by the splendid service.

> *It's very luxurious and they're very attentive to your needs, as if you are a superior being.*

He slowly got used to certain comforts and, almost subconsciously, made changes to his predispositions: he started to always be on time and it bothered him when other people weren't, he tried to dress more elegantly, even when he still didn't have the appropriate clothing to do so, he respected the traffic signs as if they were sacred,

The Sergio Torres Story

and he even started drinking tea despite staying devoted to his maté, his alfajor biscuits and his Palitos de la Selva sweets.

That first night, in the hotel, he had to share a room with centre-back Mike Williamson, one of the key players in the Wycombe team. At this point, English wasn't an obstacle for him. He understood almost everything and he spoke well enough to make himself understood. An interesting coincidence: Williamson's birthday was 8 November, the same day Sergio celebrated the anniversary of his arrival in England.

The night before, he didn't know if he would be starting, sitting on the bench or in the stands. The manager confirmed the line-up and the substitutes shortly before the match and named Sergio on the bench.

> *About 24 hours before the game, I started to get nervous. The next day, when he told me I'd be on the bench, I was very happy. It's a big step.*

He spent almost the whole game stretching on the sidelines, waiting for the manager's call that never arrived. At this point it wasn't that important. For his eyes, it was enough to enjoy the 90 minutes of the match from the side. It ended 1-1.

Two days later, but this time as the home team, Wycombe played against Cheltenham. Once again, Sergio would be among the substitutes.

Chapter 4

We played on Saturday and on Monday we had to play again because it was a Bank Holiday. There are almost always matches on Bank Holidays, but I don't understand how someone can play two games in three days. If I had to do it, I would be destroyed. They would have to drag me off the pitch and lay me down in the locker room, like that time in Mar del Plata with Quilmes.

With 30 minutes to go in the match and the score at 0-0, John Gorman told Sergio to get ready to play. He sent him to the left wing. There, in High Wycombe, seven thousand miles from his family in Mar del Plata, what he had been searching for since he had learnt to walk had become a reality: his professional football debut. It was time for him to show that he deserved to be there and that all the sacrificing hadn't been in vain.

The Sergio Torres fan club
His first play in English professional football got the attention of the spectators. He trapped the ball smoothly, dribbled towards the centre, passing an opponent on the way, then took a shot from outside the box, almost scoring a brilliant goal.

I really got a hold of it and thought it was going in. Everything was in slow motion. Right then, out of nowhere, appeared the goalkeeper's

The Sergio Torres Story

hand and the whole stadium screamed 'aaahh'. Jogging back to take my spot, I knew that if I had scored, it would've been an unbeatable debut.

On his second play the ball landed at his feet and he once again showed his skills with a few nice moves. Unexpectedly, the stands erupted with the shout "Ser-gi-o, Ser-gi-o!" Such cheering in his first game gave quite a boost to his self-esteem. His team-mates and coaching staff congratulated him in the locker room. The newspapers highlighted his performance. Wycombe played well but the result (0-0) didn't reflect that.

There would be more surprises after his impressive debut and they would start appearing just before his second match. That day, just after the warm-up, while he was heading towards the dressing room, the club photographer called him over.

> I was really focused on the game because it was about to start, but the photographer wanted me to go over to the stands. While I was walking over, I looked up and saw people wearing wigs with long, blonde, curly hair and a white headband like I wear when I play. They were dressed up like me. I couldn't believe it.

In no time, the blonde wig and white headband would become big business for High Wycombe's

Chapter 4

merchants. They were selling hoards and were making a killing. Sergio Torres had turned into a status symbol for them and the long, blonde curls were a symbol of their support for him and for the team. But it didn't stop there. In the stadium, you began to see more and more Argentinian flags, next to the English colours, and signs bearing his name.

Thanks to his solid performances, he would be among the starting 11 for their home match against Barnet on 17 September. Wycombe won 1-0 and Sergio was chosen as man of the match. He was given a bottle of champagne and had to pose in pictures with some of the sponsors. The media started talking more and more about his story and his name began to be recognised.

Big brother

It was becoming tiring for Sergio to commute from Basingstoke to High Wycombe and back all the time. He also felt bad having to ask John and Mimi if they could take him every day.

> *I quickly mentioned it to the manager. I told him that it seemed strange to me that I had been earning more money playing two divisions lower, semi-professionally. Actually I had been earning more because I was also working at Boots and with both salaries it added up. The current situation was bothering me. With even*

The Sergio Torres Story

just a little bit more money I could live closer to the training ground.

The club directors quickly found the solution to the problem. They offered to provide him a place to live with a family.

What?

They had asked a family from High Wycombe to put him up. This was not what he expected and seemed odd to him, however after seeing the house, he accepted. This is how he left Mimi and John's house for good and, once again during his time in England, he was moving. Like before, this time wouldn't be easy and he hesitated before deciding. He always had his doubts.

> *On one side, I'm happy because I won't have to cook for myself or wash my clothes, and I'm going to be able to save up a little cash as I don't need to spend much here. But what I'm worried about is that I'm losing my freedom. I'm 24, but living like a kid. I need a little privacy. At this point I would've liked to at least have even a tiny flat, but alone. Obviously I still don't have the money for this.*

Tom and Elaine, and their seven-year-old daughter Claire, were his host family, and they had a

Chapter 4

friendly little puppy named Beauty. Living with them obligated him to communicate in English all the time. He had no choice but to learn.

> *It's a little hard for me to understand Tom because he's Scottish and he mumbles, so I have no choice but to perfect my English. They are a very united family and they give me everything I need. I don't think I am causing them many problems and they are easy to live with. Furthermore, Tom drops me off at practice because he has to take Claire to school early in the morning and it's on the way. He usually spends 20 minutes at the school when he drops her off and I usually end up falling asleep in the car while I wait.*

Sergio and Claire would paint a pretty picture when seen playing and having fun together.

> *She tells everybody that I am her brother. Every time I am in the paper she cuts it out and shows it to everyone. I think she's proud of me. We play together a lot at home and we get along great.*

The Argentinian's only chore during this time was to do the washing-up after dinner, while Tom did the drying. Elaine happened to be an excellent cook.

The Sergio Torres Story

It's so good I end up eating two servings.

The house wasn't exactly close to Wycombe's stadium. Sergio had to take two different buses to get home – one to the centre and another to the house – but sometimes, fans passing by the bus stop also would offer to take him to the centre.

It's too far to walk, but sometimes I get off the bus in the centre and walk a bit because I am bored. At times, people stop and offer me a lift when they see me waiting for the bus and once in a while a team-mate takes me home, but not often because nobody lives on this side of town. At other times, somebody from the office takes me, especially the girls, who are really nice. I'm becoming friends with Sarah, Tahli and Keirina.

He was the only player on the team that took the bus to go home after practice, which made him stand out because all of his team-mates had cars (some of them were quite beautiful).

I don't even have my licence yet.

Album of the stars
The owner of Wycombe Wanderers was Steve Hayes, a rich and powerful man. He was a fanatic of Chelsea and had a table at Stamford Bridge's spacious luxury restaurant, where he and his

Chapter 4

guests could dine before the match and head down to his box for the game. Hayes could invite eight people to watch the Blues, who had one of the priciest squads in the world.

One unexpected day, he invited all Wycombe's players to join him for a match at Stamford Bridge. However, there was a catch: there were only eight spots.

I was one of the first to say 'yes'. I said 'please' over and over.

Sergio felt it was a once in a lifetime opportunity, and that's why he was so overjoyed when he received the confirmation that he was on the list of the privileged who would go to see Chelsea. He was so ecstatic that he forgot about a little problem: he would have to dress elegantly. The high society table had an image to uphold and everyone had to subscribe to it. What you appeared to have was more important than who you really were.

We had to dress up really fancy and I didn't have anything. What did I do? I called my friend Jorge Timoner and went by his house before the match to borrow some dress pants, a dress shirt and an evening jacket. I turned into a dandy.

Arriving at the stadium was as exciting for him as it would be for anyone who has worshipped

The Sergio Torres Story

football since infancy. Elegant and refined, and having shaken off the dust of the factory, he walked seriously, with his head up, but at times he couldn't hide the little boy inside and his genuine reactions. However, even in his fancy clothes, one thing didn't change. He had his camera in his hand, ready to shoot at any moment.

> *Even the surroundings of the stadium are impressive. There is a lot of history running around these walls.*

During the evening, he tried to capture every last detail so that later he could relate everything to his friends in Mar del Plata. He was entering the stadium's luxurious restaurant when the most thrilling thing happened. He squinted his eyes and saw the Argentinian striker Hernan Crespo, having dinner on the other side of the restaurant. He couldn't keep from letting out a big "wooow!"

> *I went directly over to him, and told him I was Argentinian and had come to see the match. I asked him to take a picture with me. He accepted graciously and we started to chat a bit. He stopped eating to speak with me. I couldn't believe it as he was having dinner with his family. After a few moments he told me: 'Sorry but I have to go to the locker room to wish the guys luck. I'm not playing today because I'm*

Chapter 4

injured.' He was super polite. I answered: 'Of course, of course. No problem.'

Steve Hayes and his eight guests had dinner before the match, they ate something during half-time and, after the game, those who were still hungry had something else. They were in a first-class dining room watching the rich and famous pass by.

What was I doing there?

After the match, as usual, some of Chelsea's players came over to the area where Sergio was because this is also where their families were waiting. The players that most impressed him were John Terry, one of the best defenders in the world, and Frank Lampard, one of the best midfielders in the world, both part of the English national squad.

As soon as Terry appeared, I took a picture with him, otherwise nobody in Argentina would have believed me. After that, I went to take one with Lampard. We both smiled and ... perfect. 'Excellent' I thought, but as I was walking away, I saw that the picture hadn't been taken. I stopped and thought: 'What should I do?' I said to myself: 'I'll go and ask him again,' but right then I saw that he was holding his daughter and

I didn't want to be a nuisance. But I figured that I'd never have another chance, so I went bravely over to him and apologised for the bother and, in the end, he let me take a new picture with him, which came out this time. I couldn't have been happier.

The guy from TV

Mabel and Raúl Torres started going to England regularly to be close to their son, to see first-hand his growing popularity and to even sign autographs just for being the parents of a local idol. "I was walking down the street and suddenly I looked over and saw a gigantic, almost life-size picture of Sergio inside a shop. I stood there staring at it as if I didn't know him. What was Borromeo doing there?" Raúl related enthusiastically. His wife went into a different shop and was surprised to see on display the trendy wig and headband, so she bought them.

At Wycombe's stadium, Adams Park, capacity 10,000, him mum and dad had a specially designated place from which to watch the matches and there was one thing that never failed: the Argentinian flag, with "El Coyunco" inscribed on it, had to be visible at every stadium they saw their son play at.

They hung it up or they held on to it themselves the entire 90 minutes, but it had to be there. It was very special for them to hear almost the whole

Chapter 4

stadium chanting "Ser-gi-o, Ser-gi-o", something that happened frequently.

Sergio's popularity was sky-rocketing. The biggest sports channel in England, Sky Sports, had a lot to do with this when they proposed to do a feature on him because, they told him, he broke the flashy footballer stereotype. It was a special story: two years before he couldn't even say "yes" correctly and now he was giving interviews in English.

They filmed him getting on the bus, doing the washing-up at Tom and Elaine's, and walking around town. They even took him to a shop so he could try on one of his famous blonde wigs. The feature was a hit and other journalists would begin to search him out.

During the first two months in Wycombe, my social life was almost non-existent. All my team-mates lived in different places and almost all of them had girlfriends. They don't go out much and I don't really like to go out alone.

However, the other day, some of the guys and girls that work in the club office invited me to go out for a drink, nothing more. But I was surprised to see, that at the place we went, I was like a star. Wherever I was, fans came over to take pictures with me. With me! And quite a few of them. They even asked me for my autograph. I have to admit, I'm liking this.

Boca v River

During the first half of the season, Wycombe were invincible. After the first 21 matches, they were top of the table and undefeated. As could be expected, the level of fan support rose in direct proportion to the success of the team. The rule of three can always be applied. If the ball hits the post and doesn't go in, you'll be criticised but, if it goes in, you'll be praised.

Well integrated into the squad, loved by the fans and strongly supported by the manager, Sergio was often in the starting line-up but would have to sit on the bench at times, as could be expected according to the law of adaptation. He still had to learn what English football was all about and how to assimilate into their special style of play.

> *The football here is much more physical than at home, but they don't normally have bad intentions. However, there are exceptions. You have to be tougher here. Nobody plays in the hole. Most teams play a 4-4-2 or 4-3-3. I'm starting to enjoy getting into the scramble, fighting for the ball instead of waiting for it so much. These guys are like jets. They play at 100km per hour every game, the whole time, playing strong right up to the end of the game.*

For the Carling Cup, Wycombe also started off on the right foot and ended up being matched

Chapter 4

up against the formidable Aston Villa, one of the great English clubs, and the European club champions in 1982.

This would be the first official time that Paisa would face a Premier League team. Who, in their right mind, would have imagined this two years earlier? He was discovering that dreams were still possible for those willing to dream. His fantasies remained alive, they were never-ending. New horizons were appearing to him.

The round against Aston Villa would be played as a single match. In case of a draw, there would be extra time, followed by penalties, if necessary. Only in the semi-final would there be two matches. Ninety-two teams participate in the Carling Cup, played since 1961: 20 from the Premier League, 24 from the Championship, 24 from League 1 and 24 from League 2.

Sergio immensely enjoyed that special day. It would be quite a challenge for 'El Patito' from El Coyunco, the son of Pato and Mabel Torres. He wondered what they would say in Mar del Plata and if the local radio and newspapers would talk about it. Against the team from Birmingham, founded in 1874, Sergio would enter the game from the bench with 30 minutes to go. The disappointing but unsurprising result was an 8-3 victory for the visitors.

"We were unlucky and we caught them on a good day," Paisa would write, justifying the loss.

The Sergio Torres Story

After the game, forgetting about the result, the context and that he was now a professional, he ran right over to ask Juan Pablo Ángel for his shirt. This Colombian goalscorer, now with Aston Villa, had previously played for River Plate and was in his fourth year playing in England.

> *Before heading over to him, an ethical problem arose inside me. Being a Boca supporter, I wasn't sure about asking him for it as he is still identified with River. But at the same time I wanted to have a souvenir so I went over to ask him. He said: 'Sure, I'll give it to you in the dressing room.'*

Sergio had convinced himself that it would be a nice keepsake to hold on to, but when he entered the visitors' locker room, the Colombian national player had already got on the team bus. Sergio, not losing heart, looked for the equipment manager, who was kind enough to remind Ángel about the favour. The popular striker told him to get Sergio's address so he could send it to him at a later date.

> *I gave him my address but it has never arrived. I'm still waiting. I'm actually a little disappointed, but whatever. I guess stars are like that.*

Chapter 4

Ups and downs
14 January 2006. Before the match against Notts County, John Gorman made a strange comment during his pre-game speech: "If somebody scores a goal today, please don't celebrate much." They were already into the second half of the season and, despite his great performances, Sergio still hadn't scored a goal wearing Wycombe's colours.

I heard what the manager said, but if today I finally score, you bet I'm going to celebrate.

He had been waiting a while. He was happy with how he was playing and with the team, but goals are something special and are really what football is all about. As if destiny was trying to provoke him and put another barrier in his way, his first one would come that day, the day that the manager didn't want celebrations. He scored a beautiful one, on a cold, winter afternoon, on a muddy pitch. He sent the ball, first touch, just inside the far post. The game finished 2-0.

I forgot everything the manager had said. Complete delirium. I took off running and threw myself on the ground, looking at the sky and saying 'thank you, thank you'.

The fans chanted his name for a couple of minutes, while play resumed, but the "Ser-gi-o, Ser-gi-o" seemed never-ending. Various team-mates, also disobeying the manager, joined him to celebrate his first conquest as a professional.

This was the moment he had been waiting years for and he felt on top of the world. However he wasn't aware that he would be headed down faster than he had gone up.

At the end of the match, John Gorman, the man with the strange moustache, got his team together on the pitch. They all huddled together thinking that a speech of congratulations was coming or perhaps a reproach for the excessive celebration when he had asked for restraint.

"I've got some news to tell you all in the locker room and I want us to all be together," said Gorman in an uncharacteristically soft tone.

Nobody from the squad had any idea what had happened and they walked towards the dressing room with worried faces, deducing or simply inventing hypotheses. They slowly sat down, side by side, while Gorman waited patiently for everyone to be ready before he started to speak: "Mark Philo had a car accident this morning. He passed away this afternoon."

Silence fell and soon sobbing was heard. Mark Philo, one of the players, was barely 21 years old. As he wasn't even going to be on the bench that day, the midfielder had gone out the night before with some friends. He would never return. He died in the hospital at

Chapter 4

4.20pm (Patricia Gammon, 58, also died in the accident). On request of Mark's family, the club decided to go on with the game as planned, and to inform the team members, many of them friends of Mark, after the match.

Sergio also had a good relationship with the club's young hopeful, who had been one of the club favourites and most loved players as he had been playing there since he was 15. That day, after the victory, the Argentinian would be chosen as man of the match once again, and he would end up laying the small award they gave him against the huge collection of flowers that had been left on the pitch. He couldn't understand why Mark had died because the young shouldn't die, he believed, nor do they deserve it.

All of this is terrible. This is a horrible time for us.

It was a knockout punch for the whole group, and they couldn't recover. Up to that point, Wycombe had been top of the table, but things started to go downhill fast. They began to lose on the field just as they had lost in real life.

On Saturday 28 January, before the match versus Stockport County, they held a moving moment of silence. Both teams, huddled together in the middle of the pitch, stared mutely down at the grass.

The Sergio Torres Story

The pain was strong for everybody and it was difficult to fight. There were many kind words said about Wycombe's number 14. The doors of the stadium were left open so that the scores of people leaving flowers in tribute could walk on and off the pitch freely. There was even a notebook left at the entrance for people to write their condolences. It was a tough time.

John Gorman's words of tribute to Mark Philo:
"Farewell our Darling Mark,
Prince of young players we must depart,
No more stand and admire you,
From what once was Adams Park,
So play up the Wycombe Wanderers,
Stand up and play the game,
For in a team a spirit stand,
Mark Philo is his name."

This would not be the only tragedy. The team, already knocked down and the count advancing, would receive another unfair, surprising blow. Just a few weeks later, Gorman's wife Myra would suddenly lose her fight against cancer, dying at 56 years old.

The losses on the pitch would come one after the other and Gorman fell into depression. He wanted to stay at the helm of the club despite his grief, but the club authorities decided to give him

Chapter 4

a break, arguing that he wasn't capable. Steve Brown, the assistant, took charge of the squad until the end of the season.

To top off the sad start to the year, Paisa injured his right ankle in the local derby against Oxford. This completed an ugly picture. The wheel had swung back around again.

> *I got kicked hard three times in the first 30 minutes of the match. The third one screwed me, a severely sprained ankle. I felt pain during the game but with all the adrenaline it didn't bother me and I kept playing. During half-time, I told the team doctor and he wrapped up my ankle tight so I could go out and play the second half. I played the whole game, one of my best, and was voted man of the match again, and fortunately we won 1-0. But when I went back to the locker room, I took off the tape and my ankle looked like a sausage. It was bruised and swollen, and it started to throb.*

He was told he would be out for a month. This was another big blow as his performance was beginning to peak and he seemed to be helping the team come out from under the clouds. The injury upset him and was upsetting what he was trying to accomplish after the passing of Mark and Myra. The team had hit a low spot and, with everything added up, they lost six consecutive matches, ending up in sixth place in the table but qualifying for the play-offs. The first-, second- and third-placed clubs moved up automatically while the fourth- to seventh-placed teams played for the other spot in League 1.

The idea of promotion, which seemed realistic during the first half of the season, was forgotten when Cheltenham knocked Wycombe out in the semi-finals. Sergio wasn't even able to play in the decisive games as his recovery, initially predicted to be a month, lasted to the end of the play-offs.

> *It's still bad and I don't see much day to day improvement. I go to the club at 9am and get home at 4pm, every day, but I still don't see it getting any better.*

Depression and helplessness were two new characters entering the story. He felt that he needed to somehow fight his frustration. He grabbed some scissors and started cutting off the long hair that he had been growing for more than five years. Tom helped him and, using an electric shaver, cut it short. When he went to practice the next day, his team-mates had to do a double-take to recognise him, and the club owner didn't like Sergio's look at all, as now the wig business would be pointless.

Paisa answered him: "If you had been giving me a percentage of the profits, I wouldn't have cut it."

Chapter 4

Second season

Sergio Torres and Steven Perry, nicknamed 'Pezza', met one night thanks to the girls that worked in the Wycombe offices. They all went out one night and a year later, after developing a strong friendship, would move into an apartment together in the middle of 2006. Before starting his second season as a professional, Paisa was given a raise and therefore could afford this move which satisfied his need to have his own space and more liberty.

> *The place that Pezza and I are renting has two rooms and is five minutes from the training ground and five minutes from the stadium. Perfect.*

He was fully recovered from his ankle sprain and had his mind set on playing a successful pre-season, as he hadn't played in an official match since February. A new year of football had arrived along with some changes. At the first practice, the team was introduced to their new manager: Paul Lambert.

The new manager's face was familiar to all and his name even more. Lambert had played dozens of times for the Scottish national team, with whom he had played three games in the 1998 World Cup in France. He was also well remembered for his performance in Borussia

Dortmund's victory against Juventus (3-1) in the 1997 Champions League Final, where he deftly controlled the legendary Zinedine Zidane.

In the team's first meeting with their new, fiery manager, Sergio was almost unable to participate in the discussion because Lambert spoke extremely quickly in his thick Scottish accent, and the Argentinian wasn't able to understand the majority of the ideas. Upon leaving the meeting room, he went to look for Steve Brown, who had remained with the club as the assistant coach, and asked: "Brownie, what did he say? Can you translate it for me because I didn't understand a thing."

Paisa, injury-free and without problems, had an outstanding pre-season. While he was on holiday in Argentina, he had been running in Sierra de los Padres to get back in shape, but even so he would have to wait to get back into the starting line-up. He was on the bench during the first three matches of the season but, luckily, he would start the fourth game. He scored a header to help Wycombe win 1-0, and gained his spot back in the starting 11.

The team's confidence would improve greatly thanks to the first round of the Carling Cup. They faced Swansea, a club from two divisions higher. It was an incredible match which they ended up winning 3-2 in extra time. Sergio was happy because he was playing better on the pitch and

Chapter 4

feeling better mentally. He was like a little light, illuminating dark paths for others, helping the team to play better as a whole.

The truth is that, luckily, things are going well.

Despite his confidence, the Argentinian understood clearly that he wasn't immune to setbacks. Nobody is, really. He would, once again, suffer a blow to his progress: this time injuring his knee after running into an opposing player – more precisely, a tear in a tendon at its insertion to the bone. What initially would be two or three weeks of recovery would end up being almost four months off the pitch. It was bad luck and worse timing – so much work and dedication, so many hours, days and months devoted to a result which would change in a moment, screwing everything up. He missed almost the entire first half of the season.

I have to watch the matches from the stands and, during the week, I put in more hours working out than anyone.

Revolution
With Paisa looking on, Wycombe would march strongly ahead in the Carling Cup, surprising everybody more than once: they beat visiting Fulham (Premier League) 2-1, later on penalties

they beat Doncaster (Championship), then Notts County (League 2) and Charlton (Premier League), both 1-0. For the first time in their history, the club went to the semi-finals. David became Goliath and was standing among the giants; the other three teams being Tottenham, Arsenal and Chelsea. Coming up against any of them would be a momentous occurrence.

The quarter-final match against Charlton was played on 19 December. When Sergio saw that Wycombe were going to the next round, he immediately decided to change his training method. He wanted to be ready for the coming match without a doubt, because it would be unforgettable. The lengthy injury recovery time was dampening his spirits and they assured him that, even if he did everything exactly right, he wouldn't be ready for either of the matches (there was a home and away match in the semi-finals).

He was getting sick of the same old dilemma: what you can do and what you can't, sanity versus madness, what you should do and what you want to do, responsibility versus irresponsibility, the correct versus the incorrect, many things running through his head. He had to test his knee, ignore the pain and pray to God. To get unprecedented results, unconventional things had to be done.

Sergio's mother, father and sister came to England to spend the holidays with him. Just a few hours after they arrived, the draw was done

Chapter 4

to see who would be Wycombe's opponents in the semi-final of the Carling Cup. The week before, everyone in the club was pretty nervous, but things got mad when it was confirmed that, on 10 January, Chelsea would be visiting, bringing with them players like Ashley Cole, Lassana Diarra, Claude Makelele, Frank Lampard, Michael Ballack, Didier Drogba and Andriy Shevchenko. Then, on 23 January, Wycombe would be headed to the magnificent Stamford Bridge, where Paisa had visited shortly before and had taken pictures of the monsters that had seemed untouchable.

Don't tell me I'm going to miss this dream because I'm injured.

There was no time to waste. He went directly to the team doctor and lied. He didn't normally do this but he didn't care. Sergio told him that his knee didn't hurt any more and that he felt fine. Because of this little lie, which was considered hard truth, he started jogging and doing ball work. When he got home, after a long day of specialised exercises, his mum and dad would massage the knee area to loosen it up and, perhaps in some way, aid in rehabilitation. He didn't know if, scientifically speaking, it would really help, but he had to throw all his coins into the wishing well and hope for luck.

The Sergio Torres Story

At the beginning of the last week of December, he started training with his team again. It had been four months since the last time and it was 15 days from the big day. He had only two dates on his mind: "The 10th is the first match and the 23rd is the second. I have to make it."

Saturday 6 January, 96 hours before the first match with Chelsea, Sergio would smile again. Lambert decided to make room for him on the bench in the league match against Rochdale, and he would send him on with 20 minutes left. He was back, even if a bit insecure. There were always hesitations, but as everybody knows, the only sure thing in life is death, but it's still scary.

I didn't know how I would perform or how my knee would respond.

He was well received by the fans. The game would finish a 1-1 draw, although it felt to him like a landslide victory: that 6 January, 'Three Kings Day' [a holiday held every 6 January in Spain and many Latin American countries during which the 'Three Wise Men' bring presents to all the children], he hadn't noticed any problems with his knee. Perhaps this fortunate development was a present from Melchor, Gaspar and Baltasar. They were magic kings and surely had tricks to shorten the time of any recovery, or perhaps, the unthinkable had simply occurred once again.

Chapter 4

The manager, seeing that the Argentinian was fine, in a huge gesture of confidence, put him in the squad for the match versus Chelsea. Yes, he would be playing against one of the best teams in the world and against various stars that had shone only a few months before during World Cup 2006, in Germany. The kid from the brick factory would be going at it with Ballack. The drop-out physical education student would have to run with Drogba. The skinny guy who had to get a job stocking cosmetics at a distribution company would have to face Lampard. This madman, that had come to England at 22, thinking he could be a professional footballer, would be trying to mark Shevchenko and dribble past Makelele – all because he had a dream he wanted to fulfil.

Chelsea are coming
When Paul Lambert got the squad together to tell them the starting line-up and who would be on the bench, Sergio was shaking, breathless. The moment that he heard his name, confirming that he would be among the substitutes, his breath came back. The manager had faith in the Argentinian, and it was a big deal because it had been less than two weeks since he had started practising with the rest of the team after four months out. In Wycombe's stadium there would be 10,000 people waiting for the starting whistle.

The Sergio Torres Story

It was incredible, like a revolution for the club. The giants that are Chelsea are in our house.

Shortly before heading out on to the pitch, the manager asked the players to sit down in the locker room for five minutes. Only five minutes. There was a projector and a big screen, and everybody had their mouths shut when images started to appear: goals, pictures and other plays by their team were voiced over by Al Pacino's speech from the film *Any Given Sunday*. There were watery eyes, goose flesh and butterflies in the stomach, and finally a big group hug strong enough to prepare them to head out into battle against the Roman Empire.

Line-ups
WYCOMBE: 31 Batista; 4 Martin, 6 Williamson, 5 Antwi, 29 O'Halloran; 7 Betsy, 15 Doherty, 8 Oakes, 10 Bloomfield; 9 Easter, 16 Mooney. **Substitutes:** 32 Young, 3 Palmer, 22 Sergio Torres, 28 Anya, 18 Dixon. **Manager:** Paul Lambert.

CHELSEA: 40 Hilario; 14 Geremi, 20 Ferreira, 5 Essien, 3 Ashley Cole; 13 Ballack, 4 Makelele, 12 Mikel; 24 Wright-Phillips, 21 Kalou, 18 Bridge. **Substitutes:** 41 Ma-Kalambay, 33 Morais, 49 Sinclair, 47 Sahar, 8 Lampard. **Manager:** José Mourinho.

Chapter 4

José Mourinho, the highly valued Portuguese manager, appointed from Porto (Portugal) in 2004 after winning it all, had decided that for the first leg he would put a mix of the usual starters and substitutes on the pitch. The difference in category between the two clubs was immense and, on paper, in theory, Chelsea's second and third team should be able to beat Wycombe's first-choice 11 with no problems. At the end of the first half, Mourinho, one of the best managers in Europe (UEFA had named him Coach of the Year in 2002/03 and 2003/04), seemed to be right. The visitors, thanks to a goal by Wayne Bridge, were leading 1-0.

There were still 45 minutes left, eternal or flashing, depending on how you looked at it. Einstein explained this relativity of time with a simple example: he said that when you are sitting with a beautiful woman for two hours, it seems that only two minutes have passed, and when you sit on a burning stove for two minutes, it seem like two hours.

Sergio would have given away his pay cheque to enter the game. Some things are worth more than money and sometimes just a few minutes are worth more than all the time in the world. Facing Chelsea was more valuable than any amount of money, but, while the seconds ticked past, he was still waiting on the bench for his chance.

Eventually, Lambert sent Paisa to warm up. He smiled and jumped up obediently. In a few moments, he would find himself running alongside Frank Lampard, who was also a sub and hoping to go on.

> *I looked at him and the only thing I could think was: 'Wow! I'm running next to Lampard.' Not long ago, I had gone up to him like a child, asking for a picture, and now we were warming up together.*

There were 16 minutes remaining and it was still 1-0. Lambert decided it was time and called Sergio to go on. This was his moment. There was no past, present or future. There he was, next to Mourinho, waiting for his team-mate Bloomfield to come off. He entered the pitch remembering that the biggest losses happen when you don't take risks.

Those 16 minutes

He settled in on the left and, the first time he touched the ball, Makelele would greet him in midfield. The French international player, born in the Congo, gave him an eyeful of cleats as a souvenir, but Sergio wouldn't give too much importance to the incident. He wanted to have fun, play his game. This was his goal. Perhaps all the sacrifice had been only to enjoy this match, so he needed to take advantage. Possibly this is why, on his second touch, without hesitating, he flicked

Chapter 4

the ball over Ballack's head. This was the man that a few months before, in the World Cup, had been the captain of Germany, who had eliminated Argentina in the quarter-finals on penalties.

I don't think the German liked it too much because just after, he gave me a good elbow.

His presence in the match seemed to give Wycombe a bit of luck. A few minutes after he entered, Jermaine Easter would leave the spectators astonished, equalising with an amazing goal. No, unlike the predictions, the scoreboard couldn't lie – Wycombe 1 Chelsea 1 – and neither could everyone's reactions. Lambert jumped up, shook his arms in the air and ran around celebrating. Mourinho, who during the second half had been pacing back and forth in his coach's box, sat down with a worried look on his face. The stadium went berserk.

A curious shirt exchange
During the game, Sergio had asked Makelele for another souvenir, something other than his cleats. As soon as he heard the referee's final whistle, apart from being overjoyed, he ran over to the midfielder from the World Cup runner-up French team.

After giving me his shirt, he said: 'Give me yours.' I froze at first and then gave it to him.

While I was taking it off I was thinking: 'Why does he want my shirt? Maybe to put it on his dog or something. Where's he going to keep it? I'm going to put his in a huge frame. What'll he do with mine? At least I can say "Makelele asked me for my shirt."'

A date at Stamford Bridge

On the bus ride to the stadium for the second leg, Sergio thought about his life. The brick factory. The frustrated attempt at being an accountant. The school where he tried to become a physical education teacher. C.A. Quilmes on Luro Avenue. The teasing he had to put up with for deciding he wanted to play professional football in Europe at 22. The unconditional support of his family anywhere, any time. The dream he had never had while sleeping. His friends that supported him although they thought it was absolute madness. The word "impossible", forgotten. Roland's house and the days when he had to share a bed with a snoring guy from Cameroon. Boots and having to get up before daybreak. England's freezing weather which made it harder to stand not having a home or a hug. England's freezing weather showing its face on the bike rides to and from practice and work. Being hungry and not having a pound extra to spend. Tears that could have filled a bucket. The distance and the nostalgia. The difficulty in understanding a foreign language.

Chapter 4

The rejection and loneliness that hurt. The painful remarks. The labels that stuck achingly to his body. All this, plus more, travelled with him towards Stamford Bridge, where he would play against Chelsea.

Line-ups
CHELSEA: 1 Cech; 19 Diarra, 5 Essien, 6 Carvalho, 3 Ashley Cole; 4 Makelele; 12 Mikel, 8 Lampard; 13 Ballack, 7 Shevchenko, 11 Drogba. **Substitutes:** 40 Hilario, 18 Bridge, 21 Kalou, 24 Wright-Phillips, 33 Morais. **Manager:** José Mourinho.

WYCOMBE: 31 Batista; 4 Martin, 5 Antwi, 6 Williamson, 18 Golbourne; 7 Betsy, 15 Doherty, 8 Oakes, 10 Bloomfield; 16 Mooney, 9 Easter. **Substitutes:** 32 Young, 3 Palmer, 22 Sergio Torres, 25 Stockley, 28 Anya. **Manager:** Paul Lambert.

In all of Argentina, the match would be transmitted live on ESPN. People that had forgotten about him would be surprised to hear the news and turn on the TV.

"I can't believe it. That's the blonde kid that used to live at the foot of the Sierra de los Padres. Do you remember? There, in the country."

"Yes, that's him. Pato Torres's son. The little guy that used to come pick up soil in the truck."

The Sergio Torres Story

"Who's playing against Chelsea? The twerp from the factory?"

"Is that Paisa? It can't be. What's he doing there? Not long ago he was stuck here in Quilmes. How long has it been? One year? Two? Three maximum."

"That's Sergio, I'm sure. He studied Phys. Ed. with me and look where he is. He was always saying his dream was to play professional football."

"That guy went to high school with me, but ... what's he doing on the pitch with Chelsea after being rejected here and having to work in the brick factory with his old man?"

In Mar del Plata, his family and friends, who were more up to date with the story, had gathered around the TV to see him surrounded by stars in that impressive stadium. Hypnotised, they held their heads in disbelief because who they saw on the screen was none other than El Patito, Paisa, their son, or cousin, or nephew, or just Sergio.

On the other side of the Atlantic, his old workmates from Boots, who were also watching the match on TV, would be puzzled, thinking that just the other day they had been moving boxes together with him. Keith, who was watching the match in a pub in Basingstoke surrounded by Chelsea fans, was loyally cheering on his friend.

José Mourinho had learnt a lesson on the first leg so, for the second leg, he decided to start his

Chapter 4

strongest 11. The stadium was full for the match. There were nearly 42,000 spectators, including 6,000 Wycombe fans.

Sergio, during the pre-game warm-up, looked up at the full stands. He had never played in front of such a crowd. Stamford Bridge was so immense that you would have had to multiply the population of Sierra de los Padres by 25 to fill it.

It's madness playing with so many people watching.

He didn't know how to act that night. He felt that it was a once in a lifetime experience. Among the crowd he had his own little section: in attendance were his mother, his father, his sister, Mimi and John, Pezza and Elaine. However, he had no idea where they were seated and he wasn't able to spot the Argentinian flag with "El Coyunco" written across it, which obviously had made the trip to Stamford Bridge.

Those 30 minutes

The players from both teams gave it their all the entire match, but this time the play wasn't equal. Chelsea, hungry for victory and with their first-choice starting 11, outplayed the visiting Wycombe Wanderers. Before half-time, they were already ahead 2-0 thanks to two goals by the deft Ukrainian Shevchenko. Game over.

There was still slight hope for a comeback. At least that was what Sergio thought, and why not? He had toiled against more serious challenges in the past and had come out on top.

Fifteen minutes into the second half, his manager called him over. He would be going on to play against Chelsea, in their house. The only instructions Paul Lambert gave him were: "I want you to have fun out there. Enjoy this moment."

And that's what he did. Only a moment after entering, his first move was to flick the ball over the head of Diarra who immediately took the Argentinian down with a tackle, giving Wycombe a dangerous free kick, which almost ended up as a goal. Paisa, in his element, would have more gifts for the crowd. In the middle of the pitch, after one of his team's corners, he would repeat his previous move, but this time without so much success.

> *The ball came in the air, and out of the corner of my eye I saw one of Chelsea's players coming, so I gave him a fake and then flicked it over his head. Then I realised it was Drogba, and that he was stumbling and ended up on the ground. I almost started laughing but then I saw Shevchenko coming at me. He cleared the ball away from me and it ended up at the feet of Lampard, who put it in our goal to go ahead 3-0.*

Chapter 4

Despite the mistake, unpardonable for any manager, Sergio was enjoying every moment. He was overflowing with happiness. It was his moment and life is made for moments like these. As the minutes on the scoreboard ticked by, he was overcome by the sensation that nothing else mattered. Afterwards, he would try to explain it in words while writing in his diary about that 23 January.

> *Drogba was the one who surprised me most. He's a beast. Unstoppable. But anyway ... during the game I kept asking for the ball and tried to play like I was in Mar del Plata, but I was quickly reminded of where I was during a time stoppage due to injury. There, with nothing to do, I looked around me to pass the time until play resumed. I looked up into the stands and saw thousands of people. I looked to my right and saw Lampard, Makelele and Ballack. I looked to my left and saw Essien and Ashley Cole. I looked in front of me and saw Drogba and Shevchenko. I just looked and thought: 'What am I doing here?'*

In one single play, he repeated the same move two more times: first with Makelele and next with Ashley Cole. In 30 minutes, he had done it four times in total, winning his own personal game which was defined by smiles, not goals. However, it would be a 4-0 victory for Chelsea, with the masterful Lampard scoring a second.

Mourinho said: "They weren't afraid of Chelsea or Stamford Bridge. They were absolutely brilliant. They played to win and fought for their dream. They've displayed a fantastic attitude. Congratulations to Paul Lambert and his players. It was difficult for us and we had to play seriously."

Bonus track

"Sergio, come with me, somebody wants to say hello."

"Huh?"

In the locker room, Wycombe's captain, Tommy Mooney, came to find him in the showers to introduce him to three men who were dressed elegantly in shiny suits. Paisa greeted them politely, shaking hands with each one.

"You're a great player and made quite an impression when you came on."

"Thank you very much," Sergio responded, and he went back to finish changing.

I had no idea who they were. When they had left the locker room, I went to ask my teammate: 'Who were those guys, Tommy?' He said they were the three best friends of Roman Abramovich, Chelsea's multi-millionaire, Russian owner. He also told me that one of them is Abramovich's right-hand man. I almost died

Chapter 4

right there. What an honour to be noticed and praised by Chelsea!

After getting changed, Wycombe's entire squad were treated to dinner at the stadium and were congratulated numerous times. Just before, Sergio had reunited with his family to revel in their pride of him and enjoy the infinite hugs they had been saving for him. Paisa, still a bit giddy, remained surprised by the words he had heard from Abramovich's friends.

Maybe they're still watching me. You never know. The future isn't decided. It would be another dream. And if I ended up playing for Chel…? No, please. Let's not start again.

Chapter 5

"Popular culture speaks of a race. They say you have to finish to be successful. This is a lie. We don't live to win. We live to live."
                                        Eduardo Galeano

THE ONLY thing standing in the way of Sergio's happiness was himself. Once he got past his hang-ups, he could continue climbing up the professional football ladder because it was his right, and furthermore he was finding himself in the position to do it. However, at the same time, he could be a sad winner or a happy loser; unhappy playing third division football, or satisfied with playing for a fourth division team. He just needed to figure out which option gratified him more.

The new team publicity for the 2007/2008 season reminded him daily of his reason for living. Wycombe's team shirts had the word "Dreams" written across them because it was the name of the bedroom accessory company sponsoring the club.

Chapter 5

He would wear this word stamped on his chest every time he stepped onto the pitch for practice or for an official match. Those six letters kept him from forgetting how he had got to where he was.

Paisa himself was also a marketing object that season. They were selling light blue and white Argentina shirts, with the AFA shield on the front and "Torres" written on the back. Calendars and posters with pictures of him were also for sale, in addition to the magazines featuring exclusive interviews – one in which they asked him what the first CD was he had bought and he answered: "One by Leo Mattioli."

Signing autographs was one of his favourite things. He would stop for minutes at a time to sign, trying to please all of his fans. "The club published a calendar with pictures of the players and Sergio was one of the most sought out to sign it. I watched him stop patiently for every fan, and I didn't want to be left out. I also went up to him with mine and asked him to sign it for me. Something to hold on to," Raúl Torres proudly narrated during one of his trips to Europe.

Each trip to visit Sergio got better for his parents. One time, thanks to the generosity of Steve Hayes, Wycombe's owner, they would spend a day being treated like royalty. Steve sent a limousine to the airport to pick them up and then drive them around the centre of London. Raúl would later tell the story: "It was wonderful.

Us cruising around London in a limousine, but the problem was that we couldn't understand the chauffeur at all. Think about it. I don't speak any English and not really that much Spanish either. I speak 'El Coyuncan'. Luckily, they had given us a telephone, so every time we wanted to say something to the driver, we called Sergio and passed the phone to the front. Our son would tell him where to take us and later would translate what the chauffeur had said."

Just like during his first two seasons with Wycombe, Sergio would wear number 22 – the number associated with madness. A coincidence, they say.

Beating heart, trembling body
Despite all the present confusion Sergio was experiencing, he was sure about one thing: returning to Mar del Plata when his football career was over.

"And if you meet a girl in Europe?" his mother Mabel asked innocently.

"Mum, don't worry. I'll come back to live in Mar del because I've never been taught to fall in love."

At 26 years old he seemed to have everything clear, and he justified his words by saying he knew nothing about love. His practical, but philosophical, analysis would go to pot when an angel from on high would shoot him with an arrow.

Chapter 5

Lena

Wycombe's squad travelled to Germany for part of the pre-season to prepare for the demanding year. Paul Lambert, who had made a name for himself with Borussia Dortmund, had contacts there.

> *We stayed in SportHotel, near Dortmund. It's the same hotel where the Spanish national team stayed during the first part of the World Cup last year. I got the room where Marcos Senna had stayed. We had single rooms, super modern. A luxury. Double bed, living room and even rotating plasma TV in the wall, so you could watch it whether you are on the sofa in the living room or lying down in bed.*

There were plenty of places to visit but just one thing to focus on: put in a maximum effort and finally secure promotion. He wanted to continue his progress in English football and play in League 1 with Wycombe. He believed it was time for him to make the move up. He had the experience, the support and the skills, and he had improved his physical and mental strength. However, Cupid doesn't care about timing or location.

A casual conversation between two strangers would be the spark for a difficult-to-extinguish fire.

"Are you Spanish?" one of the concierges asked Sergio on their first day there.

The Sergio Torres Story

"No, I'm from Argentina."

"Ah, OK. I'm Spanish, but I've been here a long time."

"Very good ..."

The young Spaniard's name was Miguel, and that simple moment would become more valuable than all the gold in the Vatican when he, in perfect German, called back to his workmate saying something like: "Come here. I want to introduce you to someone."

Lena Schlee was the name of the woman working behind the desk. She was wearing a green blouse and elegant grey trousers. She came over and looked up at Sergio, who immediately fell under her spell. Her big warm eyes seemed to be able to trap anyone. Sergio, although not being the sensitive type, was captivated, shattering his philosophy.

Love began to seem like teenage fear. He didn't know how to dominate it. It had arrived unannounced, entered his eyes, settled into his body, and had erased all previous moments. After that introduction, even a breath from the girl would cause a hurricane. Even the most trivial word spoken would be analysed and studied extensively, and hundreds of unnecessary hypotheses would be created from nothing. He would make up any excuse to see her. The girl with the most beautiful of names, Lena, would inspire him to write delightful passages of poetry,

Chapter 5

despite not being much of a writer or having read many books.

From that moment on, Sergio would start acting like the typical person in love. He wanted to know everything about her: Did she have a boyfriend? What was her family like? What things did she like? What was her favourite type of music?

Love is risky and he was prepared to take risks for the lovely Russian, who had moved to Germany with her parents when she was 11 years old.

Everything at this stage was new for him. There was an existing conflict that wasn't mentioned in the manuals: the tendency to embarrassingly cast his glance away when what he really wanted to do was kiss her shadow. How was he to admit that something was happening inside him? Was he going to accept it or ignore it, and what would be the consequences of each choice? Was it worth getting excited about? It was like a complicated guessing game, but with Lena he would find all the answers.

> *I don't know what it's like to have a girlfriend. I've only had one, when I was 18, but never again. It was like puppy love and only lasted three months, and since then I've been alone. I don't know if I'm in love right now.*

The Sergio Torres Story

Love was what authorised him to act foolishly without realising it. People from the outside would be entertained watching the silly things he did as a result of his blind love. It also caused the usual odd occurrences: planning what he was going to say but later, face to face, talking nonsense or simply not speaking; worrying about others taking something that still wasn't his; causing pain to the other because of their mutual love; fighting like in a war although desiring to be together in the trenches; fear of taking the first step or simply not acting how he would around any other woman. Paisa, suffering many of these symptoms, still wasn't aware that, in front of him, he had what could be another part of his life, and he had found it so far away.

> *From the first day, and during the whole week, I always 'happened' to be by the reception desk to chat with her. She spoke English very well. When I passed by, I always looked into the office to see if she was there. At times I was lucky and we would make eye contact. Sometimes, she wasn't there. After a few days, I figured out what time she arrived and what time she left, but there were some days that she didn't come in and I got a little worried. I didn't know Miguel well enough to ask about her and I saw a few team-mates hitting on Lena, but I preferred not to say anything. For two or three days,*

Chapter 5

after learning her work hours, I went walking around the neighbourhood right at the time she should have been arriving to see if I could find her. But without luck. Later I found out that she drove to work and parked in the hotel car park. I had walked around for nothing, but at least I got to know the neighbourhood a little bit. There were some nice houses.

The next step would be to invent a childish excuse to steal, at least, her e-mail address. Human beings are so strange at times and need an excuse to communicate or to relate with each other. That e-mail address, written on a piece of paper and tucked away like a sacred manuscript, would be convincing proof that the angel, who sometimes screws up, had got it right this time. Further down the road, months later, the two would become one.

Blonde Maradona

I came on for the last 30 minutes against Oxford United and the 0-0 on the scoreboard seemed unchangeable. Five minutes after entering I received the ball with space, I passed one guy, then another, then a third. When the keeper came out, I tricked him too and ended up in front of the goal alone with an easy shot. It was spectacular. My best goal since being in England. Unfortunately it was only a pre-season game and it doesn't really count, but at least the manager saw that I was in good shape, and that I want to be part of the starting 11 and have a big year.

This would be the year where he would reach his best level with Wycombe Wanderers. He began the season as a starter and wouldn't have to wait too long before scoring a goal wearing their colours in a competitive game. In Wycombe's third league match of the season, thanks to a goal by the Argentinian, the team beat Bury 1-0 in front of a home crowd of almost 4,000 at Adams Park.

He was once again taking all the right steps. That year he played in 44 league games, starting 38 of them, and scoring five goals. Although Wycombe would be eliminated quickly in the FA Cup and Carling Cup, the club reached its objective of qualifying for the play-offs, finishing sixth in the league.

The only stain on his season was another injury, once again his right ankle. It was February of 2008.

I screwed up the ankle ligaments and sur-rounding muscles again. This time we went to a specialist, and after various tests they told me that I could keep playing but I would need

Chapter 5

injections and then surgery at the end of the season. In the back part of my ankle there is a little, loose bone which is causing the pain, and they need to take it out.

He was only off the pitch for four weeks and it was during this time when the club offered him a contract renewal, as his present one was expiring in the summer. Wycombe wanted to keep him for two more years, but he wasn't completely sure.

I want to try towards playing in a higher league. I've heard there are big clubs interested in me. On the other side, I've learnt to love this club, the fans love me and I get along really well with my team-mates and staff. Wycombe is assuring me a professional contract for two more years, and this gives me a lot of security.

Choosing the sure road was one option. The risky second alternative was dreaming about playing at a higher level and hoping that the rumours of offers would become confirmations. He ended up going with the first, and would sign the new contract during a small ceremony in the centre of the pitch, during the half-time of a match, with all the fans chanting his name. He sealed an alliance that went further than just football. It was a beautiful scene.

The Sergio Torres Story

Vertigo

Lena, further demonstrating her loyalty, made the trip of around 400 miles to be with Sergio during his ankle surgery. Distances always seem shorter when there is a loved one on the other side.

> *That's how she met my parents. Mum and dad also came to England to help me after the operation and they met Lena. I had already talked about her a lot. They also came because they knew that, this summer, I wouldn't be able to go home.*

With the season over and the surgery successfully completed, it was holiday time. While he was recovering from the operation, Paisa went to northern Germany to visit Lena for a few days. Their relationship remained fairly informal, as if formality still hadn't been granted the visa to enter. They saw each other every four to six weeks. She would go visit him when she could, and he would go see her when he was injured or if the club gave him a weekend free. The couple's future was uncertain, although Cupid was very sure about what he had done.

During this particular visit to Germany, the phone would ring and the voice on the other side would offer the Argentinian a stepladder: Peterborough United, a team that had just moved up to League 1, were very interested in signing

Chapter 5

him for the coming season. This time it was more than rumours. They were serious.

A million things started running through my head. I love it here at Wycombe and it would be a big shame to leave. The fans love me, I've just signed a new contract and I don't want to let them down.

The lift had been installed. Now it was up to him to decide if he was going to stay on the same floor or move up a level, defying vertigo. Of course, the higher you are, the harder you fall. What was more important? Moving up a division and continuing to chase his dream of playing at a higher level, or staying in a place where he was very happy? Why should he leave Wycombe if he was happy there? People don't usually do that. Or perhaps they do, to avoid the possibility of something going wrong. A poor farmer from Ecuador once said that a story can be beautiful, bleak or disastrous depending on the way it ends.

Sergio wouldn't try to make this decision alone. He consulted with his family, with Lena and with the club. Wycombe's directors told him that if he really wanted to move up, they wouldn't stand in his way and would agree to sell him.

Perhaps I'll be sorry in the future but maybe I'll never again have the opportunity to play in England's third division.

He had already played at the eighth level of English football, at level six and then three years in the fourth division. It was only a difference of one level and he would have to say goodbye to something lovely that he had built with hard work. He wanted to go higher, but the height scared him. He found it difficult to fly without wings. It was like starting a new dream that could turn into a nightmare. He would consult with reason to decide, because it was important to analyse all sides, this time, taking into account the advice he had received from his parents and Lena. He finally accepted the offer, and Peterborough and Wycombe would later work out the transfer details. Once again, Sergio was defying the odds and moving up another rung, but he still didn't know if there would be a positive result.

> *I'm really sad, but at the same time very happy. I'm really looking forward to the challenge. I feel good, but I feel bad for having to leave Wycombe like this, without saying goodbye to the fans that have been so good to me since day one.*

Back to dreaming

July 2008. With the verbal agreement made, Paisa would travel to Peterborough, a city in the east of England, not far from Cambridge. Waiting for him in his new club's stadium was his new

Chapter 5

manager: Darren Ferguson, son of the legendary Sir Alex Ferguson, Manchester United's manager.

At that first meeting, he told me that he wanted to play me on the right wing. I told him that I had played there only a few times and that I liked the left or the centre more.

Later they took him to see the training facility and when they returned, they signed the papers that would officially convert him into a Peterborough United player. Another challenge, and only two steps from the Premier League.

Along with the change of club, he would also have to change houses. He had already lost count of how many times he had moved. Russell Martin, one of his team-mates at Wycombe for the three years, had also signed for Peterborough and was already renting a house in the city. He lived with his girlfriend Jasmine and, since they had three rooms, they offered to let Paisa live with them for a while, at least until he had found a place he liked.

A couple of weeks have passed and the truth is I haven't been looking around too much for a place. I haven't really thought about it because I'm so comfortable here. Russ told me it wasn't necessary for me to leave and said I could stay with them until Lena arrives. I accepted. Jazzi cooks very well. Her speciality is baked

> *potatoes and vegetables. Russ and I take turns doing the washing-up, but he is a little lazier than I am. He does only two days, and I do five.*

Sergio was getting sick of always having to mend things and he would have liked, even if only once in a while, to live a normal life; take it easy for a few months and stop dreaming. If his mission was already accomplished, it wasn't really necessary for him to feel the impulse of progression so often, which was causing him to keep falling down and getting back up. It was disconcerting to always be unsure of the future and to constantly be on the fence between dreams and reality.

A day with Manchester United
His right ankle needed to be ready before the start of the new season. His manager, Darren Ferguson, wanted to be sure that he would have a full recovery so he told the Argentinian that he was sending him to Manchester so that one of Manchester United's doctors could take a look at it. He got in the car for the three-hour journey, heading to one of the most prestigious clubs in the world. Despite his nerves, he couldn't help chuckling to himself. It was 11 July 2008, his 27th birthday.

> *When we pulled into the parking lot, I couldn't believe the cars I saw: Bentley, BMW, Mercedes, Range Rover ...*

Chapter 5

He was treated like a star. A secretary accompanied him to one of the club's cafeterias where he could help himself to whatever he wanted.

> *I was ravenous because the trip had lasted more than three hours. I served myself and sat down. Then I saw Rio Ferdinand come in, and after him Gary Neville, Paul Scholes, Ryan Giggs and Wayne Rooney. I stared at them in surprise. They served themselves and sat down at a table close to mine. I thought about taking a picture but it would've been out of place and inappropriate. I was hoping to see Carlos Tevez, my idol from Boca, but he never came in. Later I found out that Carlos didn't normally eat there with them but usually went home for lunch.*

Paisa wanted to give himself a big hug to celebrate the moment. He wanted to scream out loud about how amazing it was to share that moment with so many stars. He belonged to Manchester United's world, even if just for a few hours. Just for that day he was a part of their elite squad, fictitiously of course, but it didn't matter.

> *Five minutes later Sir Alex Ferguson arrived. I saw him head toward the kitchen but then he turned around and looked at me. I looked away, but out of the corner of my eye, I saw*

> him walking my way. I got super nervous and prayed 'please don't come over here, please don't come over here' but then I raise my head and he was next to me.

"Hello Sergio," Ferguson confidently greeted him. Paisa stood up timidly to shake his hand. He couldn't believe that the legendary manager knew his name.

"Pleased to meet you." Once again it was the Scottish manager speaking, as the Argentinian had remained silent.

> He also asked me how the trip had been and if I was alright. Then he told me that the physio was a little busy and asked me if I wouldn't mind waiting about 20 minutes more. 'No problem,' I told him, 'I've got plenty of time.' He seemed very personable but exuded respect. Later that day, I talked with my dad and told him: 'Today I got the best birthday present ever. Sir Alex came over to greet me, introduced himself and we talked for a few moments. Is there a better gift than that?'

The day he played against Manchester United
His career continued moving ahead. At Peterborough there was no time to slow down or even a moment to change gears. To make things even more unbelievable, on 4 August, they would be

Chapter 5

hosting Manchester United. The Fergusons, father and son, matched up. Sergio would be playing against another of the football world's giants. Another dream come true.

Also that day, Sergio would make his debut in front of the home fans and, almost more importantly, would be playing in his first match since the ankle injury. And there was more. He would be sharing the pitch with one of his biggest idols, Carlos Tevez, who was wearing number ten for the Red Devils.

Manchester United's line-up (4-3-3): 1 Kuszczak; 19 Rafael da Silva, 6 Brown, 5 Ferdinand, 3 Evra; 16 Gray, 7 Fletcher, 2 O'Shea; 17 Nani, 10 Tevez, 9 Campbell.

During his pre-game speech, Darren Ferguson mentioned Sergio as part of the starting 11, but made it clear that he would only be playing the first half. At the same time, the manager told him that he wanted to see him play on the left side, the spot where the Argentinian was most comfortable.

> *In the tunnel, before heading out on to the pitch, I saw Tevez not far from me. I went dumb. Not a single word would come out. Later, on the pitch, during the formal greeting between teams, I shook his hand and said 'suerte' (good luck). I was overjoyed to share the pitch with my idol,*

The Sergio Torres Story

> *but it also was my debut with Peterborough, the first time wearing their colours. As if that wasn't enough, I was worried about my ankle. I had a lot to think about. Luckily, the 45 minutes I played went well and the ankle didn't bother me at all.*

About two minutes after the starting whistle, Paisa would have his first encounter with Tevez. He didn't know whether to fight for the ball or just stand there admiring him. He hesitated a moment and the former Boca Juniors striker took advantage.

> *It was like watching a movie. I started running after him, then next to him, looking at him. Him with the ball and me with nothing, and I still couldn't catch him. I looked at him thinking: 'I'm running and fighting for the ball against Tevez.' It was fantastic. But curiously, five minutes later, something similar happened, but this time it was him chasing after me.*
>
> *I played well when I had the ball, but they had it most of the time.*

Generally speaking, Sergio had a good debut. Manchester won the match 2-0. Russell Martin, Sergio's housemate and good friend, scored the first goal. Unfortunately, it was an own goal; he tried to chest-pass it to the goalkeeper and ended

Chapter 5

up putting it in the net. Darron Gibson scored the second.

The poster in flesh and blood

After showering, Paisa went out and saw Carlos Tevez signing autographs. This time he didn't waste the opportunity and, without hesitating, went up to him with the match programme. Speaking in Spanish, he asked for two autographs: one for him and one for his father. Then, he documented the moment with a picture and they stood there chatting for about 15 minutes.

> *I couldn't believe it. The words wouldn't come out, but he was more relaxed and helped me be more comfortable. He asked me how long I'd been with the team and how long I'd been in England, and if I lived alone. Super friendly. Bravely, I said to him: "Sorry for asking Carlos, but I'd love to have your shirt to remember this moment." He answered: "The equipment manager told us that we couldn't give these ones away since they are pre-season shirts and they don't have our names on the back, but give me your address and I'll send you one of mine. Write down my number and send me your address. And, if you want to come see a game at Manchester United one day, let me know and I'll get you tickets, no problem." While he was talking, I stared at him with large eyes of disbelief.*

The Sergio Torres Story

Sergio took out his phone, put the number in and pressed the green button to call. In that moment, right there, "Carlos Tevez" appeared on the screen.

> *Because he was watching what I was doing and saw the screen, he asked me: 'How is it that you already have my number?' I wanted to kill myself. 'Dammit,' I thought. I explained that a journalist had given me his number, and Javier Mascherano's, as they are Argentinians that live close to London. I thought about calling them or sending them a message but I never had the courage. He understood and saved my number. He wished me luck on the season and I wished him the same. I sent him a message the other day with my address, asking him again to send me his shirt when he had a moment. He answered: 'I'll send it to you this week, mate,' but I still haven't received anything. And then two weeks later I sent him another message asking if he had sent it because nothing had arrived, but he never answered. I tried calling him once but he didn't answer. Maybe it got lost in the mail, or maybe he really doesn't want to give it to me, or maybe he's just too busy to think of it.*

The big fall

For League 1 teams, the season started on 9 August. Peterborough would play at Southend and Sergio would be among the substitutes. He would

Chapter 5

come on with ten minutes left in the second half, for his debut in the third division. The result was not the best: they lost 1-0. His first competitive game in the starting 11 for Peterborough would come in their next match, in the first round of the Carling Cup, against Bristol City. His manager started him on the right wing. Despite the pre-game optimism, they would be knocked out of the tournament, losing 2-1.

Despite not being at his peak physically (he had only practised for two weeks during pre-season), Paisa would continue in the starting 11 for the next four matches, and his left knee would begin to feel the wear.

> *The manager told me to take my time, to let my knee rest as it had swollen up a bit. He also told me that he would take me out of the starting 11 since he had seen me suffering in the last game.*

Sergio would be back to training with the squad three weeks later, but once again, his knee swelled up, keeping him off the pitch and close to the team doctors. Something wasn't right. He wasn't able to resume play until 1 November, when he came on for the last 15 minutes of the team's 2-0 victory over Hereford.

> *I played the next four matches in the starting 11. We won three times and drew once. I played*

alright, nothing special, just alright, always on the right wing, which I don't like at all. I don't feel comfortable there. The manager has even told me that he's not too happy with my play. We had a talk and he told me he didn't like what he saw. He was taking me out of the line-up.

Paisa's head started to whirl and he got scared, bringing on an imminent depression, feeling rotten and even upset with himself. His mood got worse with each passing day. The wind was going out of his sails. He didn't fit in well with the group. He missed Wycombe. The fans there didn't criticise him but they didn't exactly make him feel loved, like with his former club. He knew they didn't know him and he would have to win them over, start all over, but he didn't like starting from ground zero.

Looking into his crystal ball, he began to see a dark future.

I'm going a little mad. It can't be like this.

He was always on the bench waiting, but never went on. Sometimes he wasn't even on the substitutes' list, and this made things worse. It was like a never-ending fall. He wanted to show the manager that he could play, but he wasn't being given the chance. He wanted to explain to his coach that he could do well, but he didn't even

Chapter 5

know if he was in shape to do it. The worst lie was lying to himself.

> *I went to see the manager a few times to ask him what I could do to get better. He always said the same: 'Keep working and you'll get your chance.' It's very weird going to talk with him. You knock on the door, he tells you to come in, you sit down in an arm chair while he's looking at his computer. He doesn't say anything for 30 seconds. I get uncomfortable. I don't know what to do, if I should say something or just wait. He's a very solemn manager, difficult to relate to.*

While he was sleeping, his anguish troubled him. He couldn't fight against the thoughts in his head. They controlled him, and he obeyed. Days went by and he stayed depressed, trying to hide his sadness, keeping everything inside. The only person he shared his problems with was Lena, but she could only help him by telephone because she couldn't get away very often to visit him. She told him to keep trying, that things would get better and that, if they had signed him, it was because they really wanted him. The long-distance relationship only added to the pain.

He didn't want to worry his family. He lied to them by saying that everything was fine and that he would be back playing soon. He didn't talk about it with Russell either, until one day, when he was on the verge of tears, he told him everything, about his internal struggle and his pains. Russell didn't know how to help him either. He just tried to cheer him up and encourage him.

Paisa felt like he had a big weight on his shoulders. Peterborough had paid a lot for his transfer and he still hadn't made it worth their while. People in the club joked with him about it, but he didn't think it was funny. His hole was getting deeper and he began to doubt if he was really that good a player. The nights got long because he couldn't sleep. He would lie down but couldn't stop thinking. He would think about the previous day's practice, what he had done and how he had done it. He fell asleep, he woke up, and then he couldn't close his eyes again. He was worrying obsessively and he started feeling tired in the mornings. He got up and didn't feel like going to practice. Matches passed by and he didn't even get on the pitch for a minute.

The day he did come on, when there were only just a few seconds left until the end, he didn't even want to touch the ball. He was scared to do so. Really scared. "Please don't come to me, please don't come to me," he thought, hiding. Panic was making its debut. The fear of making mistakes had grown along with the decrease in his self-esteem. When he got the ball in practice, he immediately wondered what to do with the little

Chapter 5

round object; something that had never happened to him before, as he had always played without thinking. He used to play by instinct, but now he was constantly worried about making mistakes.

Sergio's mind never stopped spinning, and he didn't know how to stop it and put it right again. He felt like a different person and that he no longer had control over his own actions. He felt helpless.

I swear I'm really down. This is killing me.

Be brave? How? Courage can't be purchased at the shop. He was losing control and the madness had to be stopped. He had to give up his dream. Everything had gone so fast. Among his endless thoughts came the idea of returning to Argentina. He thought about it every day because he figured he would not be able to overcome this adversity. He missed his family and friends a lot. He missed his city and the life he could have had, although it seemed like a contradiction, but going back could mean never dreaming again.

I'm going home. This is rubbish.

Going back wasn't that easy though, because he had a contract to fulfil, and Peterborough wouldn't just let him go for nothing. They had paid £150,000 for him. However, his desire to return home, whatever the cost, was greater. The dream that had saved him was now killing him, and he was trying to fight it from his knees. Beating against the walls that were closing in on him was only serving to destroy his hands. It was pointless. It was as if he was finally reaching the end of the leap into the unknown he had taken in 2003, and the landing was going to be almost fatal because it was forced.

> *I'm leaving and that's it. I'm suffering and I can't stand it any more. I just can't stand it. I can't.*

His depression had already taken over his mind. The story was over because his pen had run out of ink. He couldn't hide it from Lena any longer and had to tell her that he wanted to leave it all and go back to Argentina.

Chapter 6

"The good thing about losing is that it is never permanent. However, winning can be negative because it is not definitive either."
José Saramago

PERHAPS A psychologist would be integral in a final effort for Sergio Torres to fight for his dream in England, his last chance to pull himself out of the current that was drowning him. Sergio was young and healthy, and was a professional footballer, just as he had dreamed since he learnt to walk. He had an adorable girlfriend, a loving family and friends on two continents. He had a comfortable home, a car and he wasn't hungry or cold. He had climbed up the rungs to the third division and had left a positive impression behind him at other clubs.

However, everything was dark and empty to him, and he didn't know where to turn. He needed somebody, someone magical, to help him see things in a different way, to change his perspective.

Why would a football player need a psychologist? I don't need one. Forget about it.

It is a mystery. Why at that point, when Sergio was at the peak of his career as a professional footballer, did he feel so low? It was a contradiction. He had so many different reasons to be happy but instead was caught in the doldrums. His depression had got such a grip on him because he wasn't experiencing even those short moments of bliss that would have provided him momentary relief, and he was convinced that being on Argentinian soil was the only cure. This seemed like the easiest solution, but it wasn't that simple. A man has to be extremely brave to kill his dream.

The only thing that he knew for sure is that, one day, he would fall hard, and the idea of receiving professional help started to seem like the only option remaining before throwing in the towel. He knew that Craig Mackail-Smith, one of Peterborough's strikers, went periodically to see a sports psychologist. Feeling stuck in the corner, Paisa asked him for the number. He called the doctor and during their first conversation, without wasting any time, told him what had been happening to him during the previous months.

Chapter 6

The first thing he told me was not to worry and that he knew a lot of people going through the same thing, or even worse. I had thought it was only me and it helped a little to know that I wasn't the only one, but I don't know ... I still feel pretty alone, despite what he had told me.

The psychologist's name was Rob Fisher and he started tossing Sergio lifelines to hold on to. He was an ex-footballer who had stopped playing at 29 because he had also fallen into depression and it was affecting his play. The hard times he had gone through years before (he retired in 1986) influenced his decision to dedicate his time to acting, journalism and studying the function of the brain, one of the human body's most mysterious organs. He wanted to focus his practice on athletes, many of whom suffer from pressure and criticism by the media. Rob soon convinced Paisa that there was hope because, in these situations, recognising a problem is half the solution.

He's going to charge me £400 for six sessions of one hour. Not too cheap. I accepted his offer because, I told him, I need urgent help. The great thing is that he comes to me. I don't have to go to London to see him.

The Sergio Torres Story

The driving wind

At the end of January 2009, when Sergio was still considering the idea of going back to Argentina, Lena would leave everything in Germany to start a new life in England. The action spoke for itself. Now they would be together every day, and this would be the main reason the Argentinian would decide to continue his journey on British soil. She was like a candle lighting his way through the darkness. This wouldn't assure a quick recovery from his depression, but it definitely helped him to overcome it. Her arrival had helped him to continue moving ahead.

Living together would be the key that would allow Sergio's recovery to be successful and lasting. Love itself would become jealous at seeing them so close. Lena had given him his smile back and gave him the energy to fight. She provided him with warmth, taking away the shivering cold. She listened to him (a dying science) and continued listening to him, until everything was out. Just looking at her inspired him and gave him the desire to march ahead.

Added to the decision to stay in England and continue playing was an eagerness to get back off the ground. The voice inside his head had been telling him it was time. There was no room to step back. He was ready to wake up, and was convinced it was time to win back the approval of his manager. His last match had been on 25 November.

Chapter 6

*I'm starting to feel a little better during practice.
I'm not back to 100 per cent but improving.*

After getting his engine started, it wouldn't be long before Sergio returned to the starting 11. He had been performing well during numerous training sessions and, on 3 March, would be back in the team. They would be visiting Leyton Orient, but the real opponent would be his mind.

He was prepared to face both rivals, knowing that the day of his return would be difficult. His sessions with the psychologist had given him strength but the sadness hadn't completely disappeared and he still felt vulnerable.

Paisa was happy when Ferguson told him he would be playing on the left, where he was more comfortable, and where he performed better.

I started off confidently, like before, and this helped a lot.

Some good touches on the ball early on was always a good sign. Peterborough were ahead after only six minutes of play, thanks to a goal from Chris Whelpdale, one of the Argentinian's closest friends in the squad.

This early goal helped give him confidence, although he still wasn't aware of the elation that was to come. However, he didn't have to wait long.

The Sergio Torres Story

In the 12th minute, Aaron McLean passed the ball to me and I tried a shot towards the far post, but I kicked the ground and the ball went straight to the goalkeeper. Luckily, it slipped under his body and rolled slowly over the goal line. It was a little ugly, but I didn't care. It went in, on my first day back. I screamed like a madman. I screamed to let it all out. I had been wanting to scream for a long time but hadn't wanted to seem mad, but here I had the perfect excuse to yell and nobody could say anything. I went nuts. I didn't know what to do. It was my first goal in the third division and my first wearing Peterborough's colours. Finally, it was something positive after so much negativity.

The sun had finally come out for Sergio. His teammates went immediately to hug him and were happy to see him celebrating after he had suffered for so long. The goal was like an award for having chosen to stay in Europe and fight his depression.

I'm so happy. As soon as the match was over, I called Lena and my parents. I had to tell them that I had played in the starting 11 and, more importantly, that I had scored. I had played well and they were happy for me. I was so excited. I always get excited. We won 3-2. Russ scored the third goal. It was fantastic. Chris, Russ and me, friends on and off the pitch, all scored.

Chapter 6

We are the champions

Sergio was feeling free to come out of his cave. There were days when he still felt the anguish near, but it didn't bother him. He knew that the distress was necessary to understand his position and learn how, in time, to get past the pain. He realised, during these tough times, that fear was sometimes useful.

Four days after his official return and the victory, he was in the starting 11 again: this time in an away match against Hartlepool. Peterborough won 2-1. Things were moving ahead. Posh were also in contention for the title but, more importantly, promotion to the Championship.

Everything seemed to be going smoothly, and 72 hours later, the team would play their third game in a week with the Argentinian again in the starting 11.

> *Before the match with Scunthorpe, everything hurt. I had played two games in four days after three months of not playing a full match. My legs felt like bricks but I wasn't about to say anything. I wanted to play and, as I was in the starting line-up, I didn't want to lose my place. Sadly, it didn't turn out too well. The whole team played poorly in the first half. At half-time, losing 1-0, the manager replaced Chris Westwood and me. He could have taken anyone off, but the two of us were the easiest options.*

Peterborough mounted a comeback and won 2-1, and they were on their way to a long awaited promotion. There was celebration in the club and in the city, but Sergio wasn't able to share completely in their jubilation. Scunthorpe was the last opponent he would play against for the club and he ended up watching the remaining nine matches from the bench or the stands.

I want this season to end as soon as possible.

In their penultimate game of the season, Peterborough clinched second position and promotion to the Championship. At the end of the final match, a draw, 2-2 at home against Swindon, each member of the team was presented with a medal. Afterwards, an open-top bus drove them around the city to celebrate with the euphoric Peterborough fans who had filled the streets. The mayor, Irene Walsh, was present to extend her congratulations as well. The party, with its flags and festivities, continued until late. However, the Argentinian was experiencing mixed feelings.

> *It was a grand celebration, but I didn't feel right. It was my first real achievement as part of a team in English football and I got my first medal. I'm proud of it. I was celebrating, but not like the others. I don't feel that I've contributed much on this team. Yeah, I played a few games,*

Chapter 6

but it's not the same. I didn't feel too much like celebrating. I don't know why. I guess I'm still a little depressed, although not like before. Meeting with the psychologist is helping a lot and I'm seeing things in a different way. He's helping me to stay afloat. But I'm really looking forward to some holiday time, and travelling to Mar del Plata to see my family.

Top of the table
1) Leicester City   96 points (promoted)
2) Peterborough United 89 (promoted)
3) Milton Keynes Dons   87
4) Leeds United   84
5) Millwall   82
6) Scunthorpe United   76 (promoted after winning the play-off final)

Betrayal and cowardice
Playing in the Championship turned out to be motivating enough for Sergio to ignore his problems and enjoy where he was. It was another step up. His dream was progressing and he was just one step away from the Premier League.

Looking at the Championship table, I can't believe some of the teams I'm going to be facing this season: Derby County, Newcastle United, Nottingham Forest, Sheffield United,

The Sergio Torres Story

Middlesbrough, Ipswich Town, Queens Park Rangers, West Bromwich Albion ...

He still thought continually about football. The ball had never ceased to be a toy for him. In Mar del Plata, relaxing alongside Lena and his family, he daydreamed about giant stadiums with thousands of spectators and saw himself playing with the ball, simply playing.

His unlimited imagination, which never rested, would come up against an unexpected barrier. A call from England would succeed in changing his mood when his agent communicated to him that, according to a report on British television, Peterborough had put him on the transfer list.

> *This is a disrespectful move by the club directors and the manager. They haven't said anything to me. It pisses me off because nobody deserves to be treated this way. I shouldn't have to find out like this. It's not fair. I don't want to miss the chance to play in the Championship.*

Betrayal comes in many forms and is always despicable, although, in the business world, it is common and almost rewarded. When it becomes habitual, it is even worse and is like a form of cowardice, betraying the victim daily. Worse yet, it always seems to come from somebody close. At what point does someone begin to lose their faith

Chapter 6

in the people around them? Why does everyone seem to proudly wear a mask? Why can't people face conflict head on? Why does it seem that to function in this world one must be partly evil? Why is lying beneficial?

Why couldn't the club have looked him straight in the eyes and told him that they wanted to try to sell him? How they had done it hurt more than what they had done. He still had two years of his contract left, and that was reassuring to him, but he couldn't help worrying.

They had taken away his security and comfort, and had cast him into the shadows of uncertainty for the coming season. He would have to prove his value and hope that a solution would present itself. Sergio wasn't going to wait around though, expecting the problem to be resolved alone or feeling sorry for himself. During his last four weeks of his holiday, while he was still digesting the news, he ran every day in the hills near his home. His goal was to arrive in Europe in top shape, and show Darren Ferguson that he had made a mistake, that he deserved to play in the Championship.

He was going to keep trying and knew that nobody could deny him the right. Stopwatch in hand or ball at his feet, he didn't give up fighting for what he believed in, and tried not to think about what people might say. He would return to Peterborough and prove them wrong.

> *I'm going to fight to stay with the club, even if he doesn't want me. My head still isn't totally straight, but at least I'm sleeping at night.*

This visit to Argentina, amid the mess of uncertainty, had been different than previous ones, and it had never been so difficult to say goodbye to his family. It was more than nostalgia; there was no way to define how he felt.

Never give up

> *In Argentina, I trained like never before, but here, being on the transfer list, I don't feel right. The team just left for Portugal for ten days and I'm here with some others training with the Under-18 squad.*

His goal to make a name for himself in the Championship was so close, but so far. When the team returned from Portugal, Sergio began to train some days with the first team and some days with the youth squad, but he always gave it his all. The week before the season started, he managed to catch his coach's eye after a good performance in the last pre-season friendly.

> *He told me that I looked good. I'm slowly winning him over again.*

Chapter 6

For the first league match against Derby County, he would travel with the first team, but wasn't even chosen to dress for the game. The same thing happened against Wycombe, in the Carling Cup, and against Sheffield Wednesday, in the second league match. Finally, in the fourth league match, with Preston, and in the second round of the Carling Cup, against Ipswich Town, he would be among the substitutes, but didn't even play a minute.

> *I wanted to play, even if just for a second, to say: 'Yes, I played in the Championship.' But I didn't have the chance, and I watched the following three matches from the stands. It's obvious that they're not going to pay any attention to me here. In practice, and during matches with the reserve team, I have been playing my best since arriving at Peterborough. If they won't even put me on the bench, why should I stay? To suffer more? I want to play in the Championship, but my dream feels so far away right now.*

Fighting and losing wasn't as bad as giving up and losing. Paisa considered looking for another club – perhaps he would be happier – and Darren Ferguson gave him the push he needed to make the decision. He told the Argentinian that Lincoln City, from League 2, wanted him on loan, and that there were other clubs from the same division who were interested in him.

I think the best thing for me is to go to Lincoln. It's an interesting offer. I want to play. Things haven't been going well here at Peterborough for a while and I think the change of club, team-mates and manager will also help me psychologically.

His dream of playing in the Championship seemed to be escaping him. However, despite being disappointed with what was happening in Peterborough, Sergio was proud to have fought for what he wanted.

Hello Lincoln

His loan was confirmed on 17 September 2009 and, two days later, he would make his Lincoln debut in the starting 11, adding yet another set of colours to his list. It was a home match against Shrewsbury Town, but Lincoln lost 2-0.

He was already familiar with this league and, as before, he stood out on the pitch. But the team would go on to lose two more consecutive matches, against Bury (2-0) and Notts County (3-0). Before his arrival, the team hadn't been successful either, earning only nine out of 21 possible points.

This unprofitable situation would soon lead to a change of manager: out was Simon Clark, the man responsible for bringing Sergio to the club, and in was Chris Sutton, the Blackburn

Chapter 6

Rovers legend, who had won a Premier League title alongside Alan Shearer, the team-mate with whom he had formed a lethal, goalscoring attack. Sutton had retired as a player in 2007 and this was his first job as a manager.

> *I feel bad for Simon Clark. I liked the way he worked during training sessions, and the tactical and technical drills he had us doing. He's a great guy, but we have to move ahead. Sutton is an emblematic figure here in England, and we need to make the best of it.*

Sergio stepped up his level under the new manager and was man of the match twice in a row. In the second game, he scored the only goal in his team's victory over Aldershot Town, a team fighting for top spot in the table.

> *One of my friends here in Lincoln, Richard Butcher, a great guy, passed me the ball and I ended up one on one with the goalkeeper. I faked a shot, he went to the ground and I just jogged towards the goal. The team went nuts and we won 1-0. It helped a lot to get off on the right foot with the manager.*

The stint with Lincoln lasted until the end of January 2010. The club seemed to be effective medicine for someone who was attempting to hold back some restricting internal feelings. While he was at Lincoln, his appetite for enjoying himself on the pitch came back. In an FA Cup match, he scored another goal, during his team's 3-1 victory over AFC Telford. He was no longer controlled by his fears, which had been causing him to play timidly, and once again he had become the confident player he was before.

> *The only problem was that I had to commute from Peterborough to the training ground every day. It was 90 minutes each way. The drive back was worse because I was always tired after practice. I just about killed myself three times falling asleep at the wheel. I discussed it with Lena and we decided to move closer. Yep, another move. These moves are really tiring.*

He was rediscovering the power of the decision to be happy no matter what. Lincoln was helping to cure him and helped him realise that you don't always find happiness at the top.

The four months there were all smiles. They won some matches on the pitch, and Sergio won a championship in his mind. When he left the club, it would be bitter-sweet because it didn't end in the best way. Against Cheltenham, a 1-1 draw, he came down after a header and landed badly on his left ankle. It was a serious sprain and he would miss the games remaining on his loan contract.

Chapter 6

I've already had my right ankle operated on and now I've injured my left ankle. I can't believe the bad luck I have. I wanted to play more and demonstrate my gratefulness to them. The fans are great and whenever I am in the stands, everyone says 'hello' and encourages me, and people also stop me in the street. It's a shame I can't give them something back on the pitch.

It was time to pack his bags once again, and he would be returning to Peterborough feeling cured and with the motivation to continue chasing his undying dream. Would he get the chance in the second half of the season to finally play in the Championship?

The freedom to dream

In November, while Sergio was playing for Lincoln, Darren Ferguson left Peterborough, after reaching an agreement with the club. Mark Cooper took over until February 2010, when he was fired due to poor results. Jim Gannon was the man chosen as the team's third manager of the season and would be the man responsible for trying to avoid relegation. At this time, Paisa had come back, had completed his ankle rehabilitation and was feeling mentally recovered as well. He had learnt from his experiences.

The Sergio Torres Story

One of these days, if the manager thinks I'm ready, I could have the chance to play in the Championship and fulfil this dream. Another one. I know we are bottom of the league, but I'd like to at least come on and play five minutes.

He would give it all during practice sessions – with a red face and sweaty shirt – and his efforts would not be in vain. Gannon named him as one of the substitutes for three consecutive matches, against Ipswich Town, Swansea City and Coventry City.

During those days, his heart was beating strongly, expectantly waiting. Dreaming was still his best talent and, when he did, he felt better than at any other moment. The oasis would be seen on the horizon sooner than expected, and it would appear even more satisfying to him than ever. On the night of Tuesday 9 March 2010, the invitation he had been waiting for finally arrived.

Sheffield United were the opponents and I was on the bench for the fourth match in a row. Lee Frecklington got injured and was unable to play in the second half. The manager looked to me and said: 'Do you want to play? Are you ready?' A shot of adrenaline ran through my body and, as always, I got a little nervous. I didn't know what to do, but instinctively I answered: 'Yes, of course.'

Chapter 6

His desire to carry out his dream was stronger than any apprehension, and he perceived assurance and confidence in the manager's eyes. Sergio was making his debut in the Championship, tossing all theories out of the window and defying logic. Peterborough came away with an extremely important 1-0 victory and what had inspired the Argentinian seven years earlier came back to mind: knowing that there is always a bit of fantasy present in reality.

> *I was well received by the fans. I think some had even forgotten about me, but when I appeared, they remembered me. I think I played well, although I was booked within a minute of my debut in the Championship. Before the second half had started, I asked the fourth referee if I could come on, and he said I could.*
>
> *So I came on, play started and I made a tackle to recover the ball. The referee went to speak with his assistant, came back, and gave me a yellow card for not asking permission to enter the match. I tried to explain to him that I had asked the fourth official, and he had said yes, but he denied it and I had to accept the card.*
>
> *Luckily, it didn't matter, and it didn't spoil my happiness. The game ended and I went immediately to call Lena, and then later my family, to excitedly tell everybody that I had*

The Sergio Torres Story

made my debut in the Championship. Another dream fulfilled.

With his first appearance in the Championship, Sergio had plucked another star from the sky to add to his collection. The mad Argentinian was living another utopia. If only he could have seen himself through the eyes of the young man who arrived from Mar del Plata in 2003. With this accomplishment, his depression was forced to disappear completely. Later he would write in his diary, confirming this personal victory and saying that his dream factory had re-opened its doors after a long holiday. Welcome everyone.

Chapter 7

Moments
If I could live my life all over again,
in the new one I would try to make more
   mistakes.
I wouldn't try to be so perfect, I would relax
   more.
I would be more foolish than I've been, in fact,
I would take few things seriously.
I would be less hygienic,
I would take more chances,
I would travel more,
I would watch more sunsets,
I would climb more mountains, I would swim
   in more rivers.
I would go to more unknown places,
I would eat more ice cream and fewer beans,
I would have more real problems and
less imaginary ones.

I was one of those people who lived sensibly
and productively every moment;
of course, I had happy moments,

The Sergio Torres Story

but if I could go back I would try
to have only good moments.

In case you don't know, that is what life is made of;
moments. Don't waste even one.

I was one of those people who never
went anywhere without a thermometer,
a hot water bag,
an umbrella and a parachute.
If I could do it all over, I would live more
  frivolously.

If I could live again
I would start walking barefoot
until the end of autumn.
I would take more turns on the carousel,
I would watch more sunrises,
and I would play with more children,
if I had my whole life in front of me.

But, as you can see, I'm 85 years old…
And I know I am dying.

Anonymous

Chapter 7

Sergio Torres – matches in the Championship

09/03/10, Peterborough 1 Sheffield United 0. His Championship debut. He played the entire second half, after coming on as a substitute for Lee Frecklington. Attendance: 6,674.

13/03/10, Watford 0 Peterborough 1. Full debut. Attendance: 16,591.

Having played well on my debut, I earned a spot in the starting 11.

16/03/10, Peterborough 1 Doncaster 2. Second consecutive game in the starting 11. Attendance: 6,773.

I went one on one with the goalkeeper but he ended up stopping me. It was the best opportunity I've had to score in the Championship.

20/03/10, Nottingham Forest 1 Peterborough 0. Third consecutive start. Peterborough's opponents were one of the most important clubs in English football history and two-times European champions (1979 and 1980). Attendance: 24,582.

I played one of my best matches. In the end, we lost, although we didn't deserve it. It was raining cats and dogs. We wore the third kit, light blue and white stripes, like the Argentinian national team. A beautiful stadium with almost 25,000 spectators.

23/03/10, Scunthorpe 4 Peterborough 0. Fourth consecutive match as a starter. Attendance: 4,995.

I played horrible. It was our worst match.

27/03/10, Peterborough 0 Bristol City 1. Started on the bench and came on for Josh Simpson with 15 minutes remaining. Attendance: 6,445.

Having played poorly in the previous game, I was dropped to the bench.

03/04/10, Peterborough 2 Newcastle United 3. Back in the starting 11 again after one match as a substitute. Attendance: 12,877.

I was proud to play against fellow Argentinians like Fabricio Coloccini and Jonás Gutiérrez. I also played against former team-mate Mike Williamson, who had been my room-mate on my first night as a professional with Wycombe.
   Thanks to Mike, at the end of the game I went to the visitors' locker room and spoke for a while with the Argentinians. They gave me their shirts and Coloccini asked me for mine. I don't

Chapter 7

know why, but I gave it to him. It was great, but bummer about the match. We lost and, worse yet, the manager took me off at half-time, even though I was playing well. Coloccini asked me if I had got injured, and I said I hadn't, and that it had been the manager's decision, and he told me that I was the only player causing their team problems. This pissed me off even more, but also made me feel good hearing praise from one of the Argentinian national team players.

What happened at half-time? We were level at 1-1 and, in the dressing room, the manager recognised that we were playing really well, but then announced that he needed to change the tactics and defend the draw because they were going to come out attacking. He said that Dominic Green (who had scored) and I were being replaced. At that moment I couldn't help but let out a 'what the fuck?' Unfortunately, the manager heard me and asked: 'What did you say, Sergio?' I wanted to die. 'Nothing,' I said. 'Nothing.' I took a cold shower to calm down.

05/04/10, Barnsley 2 Peterborough 2. Back in the starting 11. In the pre-game speech, the manager apologised for taking me off against Newcastle and admitted it had been a mistake. The team needed to win to avoid being relegated. Five minutes from the end, Barnsley scored an equaliser and Peterborough were relegated. Attendance: 11,290.

> The fans applauded us and we applauded them too. It was a sad day...

10/04/10, Peterborough 1 Leicester City 2. Sergio's last match as a starter in the Championship. In the last three league games (against Reading, Blackpool and Plymouth), he wouldn't even be among the substitutes. Attendance: 9,651.

Undivided Smiles

Before the end of the 2009/2010 season, Gary Johnson replaced Jim Gannon as Peterborough's manager, aware that, after relegation, he would need to prepare the squad to compete in League 1.

A new stage was coming and his first action was to meet with each player individually and tell them what he thought.

> In the meeting with me, he told me that he didn't need me for the next season. I asked him why and he told me that I wasn't the type of player he liked and that, if I stayed with the team, I wouldn't play. I had been thinking that next year would be MY year, helping Peterborough to move back up to the Championship. I was comfortable, I felt great and I had stopped thinking about my problems from the past.

Chapter 7

The good thing is that, this time, the manager himself told me the news and I didn't have to find out through the grapevine.

Every human being has a special quality hidden inside them and Sergio had developed his during his years in England. Now it was a huge advantage. He was able to move ahead and continue dreaming without even knowing where he was going. He didn't need to plan, especially when it was necessary to improvise. He had forgotten some of his routines from long ago and disregarded predictions. The discovery that happiness can be found behind many different doors had been key for him and he no longer allowed lofty ambition to dominate his decisions of which road to take.

He still had another year left on his contract with Peterborough but he decided that it was time to move on. He needed to do away with any negativity, plant new seeds for new projects and go somewhere that reciprocated his affection.

I need to be with a team that is up front with me and values me. If I am playing well, I should play, and if playing poorly, I should be on the bench.

At this point, there were two main teams who were seriously interested in the Argentinian: the familiar Lincoln City, from League 2, and non-league Crawley Town.

The Sergio Torres Story

I want to keep playing in the Football League – the teams in the first four divisions.

There was something obvious influencing his decision. The fall from the Championship to what was effectively division five seemed too big a drop and the landing could hurt more than expected. Furthermore, he had been through a lot to establish himself in the upper divisions to later throw away the privilege. It seemed foolish to opt for the lower level club and leave vacant a space that thousands would love to fill.

Must one always act logically? How important is this logic, and who decides what is logical and what isn't? Paisa, disregarding reason, agreed to meet with Crawley's manager, Steve Evans, out of respect and gratefulness for his interest in him. However, he did it a bit reluctantly, without expectations or even motives.

I really don't know why I've agreed to the meeting as I'm not really interested.

When they sat down, Evans told him about the players that he had signed and those who were going to sign, and mentioned that an English businessman, who was living in Hong Kong, was investing a lot of money in the club. He assured Sergio that the idea was to move up, there was no question about that, and he offered him a two-

Chapter 7

year contract, one year more than Lincoln had offered him.

It was quite strange. I had intended to tell him 'no' straight away, but he managed to change my mind in a short time. I left almost convinced.

The two-year commitment, the most important point, gave him security, but not just for him, also for Lena. For the last year and a half, he had been thinking about more than just himself. Now, he was thinking for both of them, or perhaps the two of them were thinking for one. On the other hand, Sergio was already 29 years old and he didn't have a whole lot of cards left to play.

Before making the final decision, he wanted to hear the opinion of his family and of Russell Martin. "Judging by the players he mentioned, I'm sure you'll move up next year and will be playing in the league again," commented his friend and team-mate from Peterborough. In the evening, just a few hours after the meeting, Steve Evans sent the Argentinian a message asking if he had thought about it, adding that he needed to know as soon as possible or he would have to find somebody else.

He put the pressure on, and in that moment I told Lena: 'That does it. I'm going to play for Crawley Town.'

The Sergio Torres Story

On 7 July 2010, a record-breaking deal was made. Sergio Torres became the most expensive transfer ever for the club: £100,000.

Roses and thorns

There was no reason to drag out the decision. Sergio wasn't an expert in making logical decisions, but a creator of dreams. However, there remained questions to be asked: Did the descent to the fifth tier of English football really matter? Was happiness prohibited at that level? Crawley Town was his sixth English club and would also be the sixth level he would play at, having seen action in the eighth, sixth, fourth, third and second tiers of English football.

To the critical sports eye it was a step back, playing in an inferior league, and a step down for his well-conditioned legs. However, he still felt on top of the world, being motivated and playing with a smile on his face. It seemed like a contradiction but everyone is free to see life the way they want.

This time around, there wouldn't be so many TV cameras, photographers or fans filling the stands, but this wasn't really important. He had learnt to adapt to any situation and he felt prepared for the challenge. Further adding to his motivation was that he noticed right away, during the pre-season friendlies, that the manager had been serious. The squad had the right stuff to go all the way.

Chapter 7

The club has purchased something like 15 players. They're not screwing around about moving up.

I know you

With the club's permission, Lena and Sergio stayed for a month in a hotel in Crawley, while they looked for a new place to settle.

It's not so great living in a hotel. I, luckily, get to leave for a few hours a day to practice, but poor Lena has to stay there inside or walk around Crawley town centre. The days get long.

The couple was becoming quite close. Lena, with Russian roots and German upbringing, drank maté – one of Sergio's favourite Argentinian drinks – and was taking on other Argentinian habits more and more. Sergio, after becoming comfortable speaking English, was now learning German. "Back home he didn't even master Spanish and now he speaks three languages," said his father Raúl, unbelievingly, after hearing his son speaking to his in-laws.

Time was passing and Lena and Sergio still hadn't found the right place to live. Michel Kuipers, Crawley's goalkeeper, had heard about the couple's urgent search and mentioned to them that an acquaintance of his was renting a nice flat in Brighton. It was a little over 20 miles to the

The Sergio Torres Story

training ground and was on the coast. Paisa liked the idea immediately.

> *When I went to see the owner of the flat, I was shocked to see in front of me the Brighton player Adam El-Abd. It brought to mind my first trial in England, with that club, almost seven years ago. I could never forget his face. It had been him that came after me every time I touched the ball. Bald, stalky and mean-faced. At the time, I thought he was going to have me for lunch, and I told myself I would never forget him, and sure enough, a lot of time has passed, I've seen thousands of faces and his has never disappeared. At that trial, he had scared me to death, knocking me off my feet more than once. What an animal!*

"Do you remember me? You remember how you attacked me?" asked Paisa, laughing, during the unexpected reunion.

"Of course I remember, and later, when we saw that you signed with Wycombe, we wondered why we hadn't signed you. You were pretty sharp in those days."

> *Thinking about that, when I met him at the trial, I didn't have a penny and I was staying with the guys from Cameroon. Now, seven years later, I'm renting his flat. Funny how*

Chapter 7

times change. The incredible thing is that it turns out he's super nice and he's even giving me a deal on the price.

The grump

As the season progressed, Sergio Torres was able to confirm the rumours he had been hearing: Steve Evans was an explosive manager and was known for yelling and getting upset often. One explosion after another. At half-time, if he didn't like something, even the windows would shake. Sometimes Paisa responded too sharply and the manager would come back at him.

> *He's always barking orders. He screams my name 50 times a match and I can't concentrate. One time, after I lost the ball, he started yelling: 'One more, one more, one more!' I looked over and he told me: 'Next time I'll substitute you!' It really upset me and I ended up losing the ball three more times, but he didn't take me off. At half-time we had a few words, but he wanted to keep me on. My team-mates still tease me about it, saying 'one more'!*

Even during low pressure games he always seemed to find a reason to yell at somebody. He even managed to blow up during a relatively unimportant match, a regional cup tie, when both clubs were playing predominantly reserves

The Sergio Torres Story

and substitutes. There were barely 50 spectators there withstanding the minus two degrees. He went out of control and yelled at everybody, one by one.

> *The pitch was in worse condition than any I had seen with Basingstoke. Nobody wanted to be there and, on top of that, he yelled at me the whole time. He took me off with ten minutes left and we lost 2-0. I consider that day, without a doubt, the lowest point in my career.*

Paisa would eventually get used to this love-hate relationship and, although Steve Evans was quite harsh, the team were having success and continued their winning streak. On 28 August, during an away match against Hayes and Yeading, which Crawley won 3-0, Sergio scored his first goal at this level, but without too many people to witness it. There were only 320 spectators.

> *I have to be mentally tough when I go to stadiums like that, where there's barely anybody watching. It's difficult for me because only three months ago I was playing against teams like Nottingham Forest with almost 25,000 people in the stands, or against Newcastle United. Sometimes, looking around me, I want to go hide in a well, but I need to keep moving ahead.*

Chapter 7

Keep dreams alive

His professional football debut, his stand-out games with Wycombe Wanderers that made him a star, visiting Stamford Bridge to play Chelsea in the semi-final of the Carling Cup, the friendly against Manchester United and his idol Carlos Tevez, his time in League 1, the promotion with Peterborough United and his matches in the Championship, they had all formed part of a beautiful past and were carefully stored away somewhere secure, never to be forgotten. After dropping into the Conference national division, English football's fifth category, the fairy tale of walking on the clouds seemed over. He couldn't complain, or hope to freeze time.

At this point in his journey, his only objective was to continue searching for happiness. There was nothing that could distract him. It was a simple question this time: who would want to be an unhappy king?

However, he was not superhuman, and unable to ignore the little voices in his head. There was something disturbing him about where he was, although he had accomplished a lot in only a few years. He had already been wounded in battle, but not shot dead. He had stayed afloat through mighty floods. He had withstood rain and wind, lightning and thunder. He had triumphed, and he had fallen in love. The only thing missing was to write the final chapter of the story he had first imagined as a young man in Mar del Plata. He still wasn't convinced he wanted it to end. There was a looming epilogue still waiting to be written and new possibilities to discover.

Sergio started to have the nagging feeling that even at Crawley Town there could be some little surprises waiting for him, but knew that to unearth them he would need to be patient and perhaps suffer a bit more. Chasing after a dream didn't cease to have its dangers and, as always, could include fear, pain and sacrifice. Despite the risks, he was prepared, once again, to walk on the wild side. He was beginning to feel uneasy, almost too comfortable, and was yearning for a bit of madness, a new challenge. He was willing to take whatever opportunity came his way, however unorthodox it might be.

Writing history

As his past history demonstrated, the Argentinian was often surrounded by unique circumstances and other outlandish events that added fuel to his fantasies.

Matt Tubbs, Crawley's star striker, and Sergio formed a lethal duo. A large part of the Englishman's 44 goals that season were scored thanks to assists by the deft, curly-haired midfielder. They set themselves apart so much on the pitch that later T-shirts would be sold in the club shops displaying the logo "T&T" (Torres and

Chapter 7

Tubbs). Both were universally considered to be the team's lucky charms, creating an atmosphere of great expectation.

During the season, the victories added up week after week. In the FA Cup, they visited Newport County, winning 1-0 to secure their place in the first round proper, where they beat Guiseley 5-0, with Paisa scoring the fifth goal with a header.

A new page was being written in the club's history. It was to be the first time they had played in the second round of the oldest football competition in the world. History was being lived in the present, but was far from being concluded. A surrealistic panoramic was being painted and Dalí still had plenty of finishing touches yet to add.

The draw matched them up, at home, against League 1 side Swindon Town, who were the clear favourites because of their higher status. However, the explosive combination of "T&T" (assist by Torres and goal by Tubbs) produced a 1-1 draw, sending both teams to Swindon for a replay on Tuesday 7 December. This would be the day of the next great feat.

It was incredibly cold and the match was almost postponed. Fifteen minutes after the starting whistle, I noticed something that had never happened to me before. I touched my hair and it felt like I had put a pound of gel in it. It had frozen stiff. The thermometer read -4°C.

In the pre-game speech, the manager told us that we were going to play a 4-2-3-1, very attack-minded. He told me I would be one of the two in the middle. I was a little bit worried because I had never played there and was scared that I would get lost on the pitch. Luckily, it didn't happen, and I ended up playing one my best games.

We came out hard from the start and went up 1-0, but later they came back and went 2-1 up, then we equalised with ten minutes to go. The game went to extra time. The pitch was almost frozen and the bottom of almost everybody's feet were hurting. My parents, who had come for the holidays, were in the stands bundled up, fighting the cold.

Ben Smith scored the decisive goal and the team celebrated like madmen. We won 3-2 and, like heroes, we secured our place in the third round and with it a chance to face one of the biggest clubs in England. Journalists and photographers flooded into the changing room to record the event. Nobody could quite believe it. Crawley Town, a semi-professional club, were making history.

Agony before the triumph

The unbearable cold succeeded in delaying the majority of the matches scheduled in December.

Chapter 7

However, the club and the town would be stirred up by the news that on 10 January, for the third round of the FA Cup, the legendary Derby County, from the Championship, would be visiting. The game would be televised in England on ESPN, and Sergio's family would be watching it on the internet from Argentina. They would all get together at cousin Ariel's place, who predicted: "Today 'El Oveja' ('the sheep', one of Sergio's nicknames from the brick factory referring to his curly hair) will score the winning goal."

Paisa, with his therapeutic laugh that helped him imagine the impossible, was back in the spotlight. He had a clear theory memorised: however high the wall, it can be scaled. Whatever pain was caused by the barbed wire cuts, it was nothing compared to the freedom felt after the escape. He was sure that, even as a Conference team taking on a Championship team, he could reach greater heights with Crawley Town.

The confrontation with Derby County was unprecedented and he was prepared physically and mentally to play flawlessly in what could be another epic scene. He had had a few weeks to train his legs and mind to work together in unity, but his hard work and dedication would end up being forgotten. Everything would be lost when, after arriving at the stadium at around 5.30pm, he was told something devastating. Richard Butcher

The Sergio Torres Story

– a team-mate of Sergio's at Lincoln – had died of heart failure the previous night.

> *Football is nothing. It becomes irrelevant when a mother and a father lose their son. What the hell can you do? What can you say? Who do you turn to?*

After hearing the terrible news, Sergio felt like he was suffocating, and froze, exhibiting no external reaction. It took only a moment to discharge completely the battery that he had been recharging for weeks.

> *A lot can happen in a second.*

He asked, almost breathlessly, for them to clarify who had died, thinking for an instant that it had to be a different Richard Butcher. How was it possible for his closest team-mate from his time at Lincoln City to die at 29? It wasn't possible. How could this happen? But they confirmed that indeed it was his former team-mate and friend. The practices, matches and conversations they had shared appeared to him suddenly, and he felt like disappearing. He was also reminded of his cousin Sergio's death in 2004.

> *Even young people, with a lot of life ahead of them, pass away.*

Chapter 7

With these thoughts running through his head, he was supposed to be preparing for the match against Derby County. It needed to be done, for his team-mates, his manager, and for the fans, but it wasn't that easy. Paisa had to make a decision and, ignoring what one part of him was saying, he determined he would go out on that pitch and win.

Sergio's day
The teams had already taken to the pitch and the January weather was ugly: rain, wind and cold. Somehow this threw off the balance and tilted the scales towards the home team.

> *One thing we do very well is apply pressure. Teams from the Championship are used to having possession and I had felt more comfortable there. But in the Conference, everyone just runs, fights and pressures. There's no time to look around.*

Crawley Town were providing battles all over the pitch. When the match had barely started, Sergio knocked Kris Commons, one of Derby's stars, over one of the short walls surrounding the playing area.

> *It was meant to let him know that it wasn't going to be an easy night for him and that we were going to be fighting the entire time.*

The Sergio Torres Story

Broadfield Stadium had filled the stands with a record-breaking 4,145 spectators, and the first explosion from the loyal, home crowd came at the 30-minute mark, when Crawley's Craig McAllister opened the scoring. Then, with half an hour remaining in the second period, Derby's Miles Addison equalised.

At 73 minutes, I looked toward the sideline and saw that we were making a substitution. The official held up the number eight. I really didn't want to go off. It was 1-1 and we were holding our own but, on the other hand, somebody with fresh legs was going to be more effective than me. Just as I was almost off the pitch, I saw Scott Neilson down with a cramp, asking to be taken off. 'Perfect,' I thought. The manager had no choice.

The score was still level, a fact already worthy of distinction. Four minutes of injury time were added and Crawley, to everyone's surprise, didn't stop attacking. During this time, the Argentinian would be given a clear opportunity to break the deadlock. A ball was cleared and came to his feet and he took a shot which was headed for the back of the net.

Time was up and the ball was heading for the top corner, but a defender came out of nowhere, jumped up and nudged the ball over

Chapter 7

the crossbar, giving us a corner kick. I lay on the grass holding my head. It would've been the winning goal.

The corner kick itself would provide one of the moments that make life worth living. Dean Howell shanked the corner (later, during the week, rumours would say it had been a designed play), and Paisa, from the edge of the box and using the inside of his right foot, diverted the ball just inside the far post, scoring and causing pandemonium.

That moment was indescribable. I felt like God for five seconds. I took off running, I took my shirt off and spun it around my head. The whole team came over to hug me and I threw myself on the ground. The manager ran onto the pitch like Diego Maradona after Palermo's goal against Peru. It was unbelievable, really unbelievable, like a film.

That was it. Nothing more to think about. The whistle blew and the victory was sealed. Hundreds of fans came on to the pitch to celebrate and came after Sergio to hug him, kiss him, touch his hair, and lift him up in the air. He could barely move for ten minutes. They didn't let him. They praised him like a saint, like a pop star. The police even had to intervene and escort him to the dressing room. ESPN and other media were there waiting to interview him live. With the microphone in his face, his heartbeat racing and thousands of people watching, he knew exactly what he had to do. He dedicated the winning goal to Richard Butcher, and sent his most heartfelt condolences to the family.

In the spotlight
The victory over Derby County marked the border between the past and the future. There was an air of celebration at the club. The fans were enjoying being on a bigger high than they had ever experienced before and many people decided to call the day "Sergio's Day", and commemorate it every year. Sergio was back on top and feeling at his best. Thanks to his last-minute goal, and for his hard work during the entire game, he was elected man of the match and given an enormous bottle of champagne.

> *It's the biggest one I've ever seen. I didn't let it go during the entire dressing room celebration. When I got home, I set it down on the table and heard fizzing. It exploded. I wanted to die. There was champagne all over the table and the carpet. It blew up by itself.*

His phone number was passed around by all the journalists, and his mobile phone didn't stop ringing during the first weeks of ecstasy. They

Chapter 7

called him from the radio, newspapers and TV stations, from all over: England, Argentina and Spain. Surprisingly, his name and story were mentioned in far flung countries like Hungary and Bolivia, where the FA Cup isn't considered important. Even friends of Lena would find out about it through a Russian sports publication.

The Sun, one of the best-selling newspapers in the UK, made his star shine even brighter by talking about him every day, after the match against Derby County until the fourth round match against Torquay United (League 2). The first report was a two-page spread shared with Fernando Torres, the striker from Liverpool, comparing the Argentinian and the Spaniard.

> *They talked about my salary and his salary, about my car and his car. They wrote that I was renting a flat and showed pictures of his intimidating mansion. They mentioned how much Liverpool had paid for his transfer and how much Crawley had paid for mine. They compared everything. They should have commented that my team was still in the running for the FA Cup and that his had been knocked out. At least this would have been one fact in my favour.*

The well-known TV channels BBC London, Sky Sports News and Eurosport UK interviewed him more than once. Talksport, Britain's leading sports radio station, called him on various occasions. *The Guardian, The Times, News of the World, The Telegraph, Daily Mirror, Daily Mail, Daily Express* and *Metro* also told his story, not to mention the local media from Crawley, Wycombe, Lincoln, Peterborough and Brighton.

Argentinian magazines and newspapers also gave homage to "the boy that used to work in a brick factory and went to Europe with 300 dollars, to later make a name for himself in English football": *Clarín, Olé, La Nación, La Razón*, Mar del Plata's *La Capital* and *El Atlántico*, Mendoza's *Diario Uno*, La Plata's *El Día*, Tucumán's *La Gaceta* and Santa Fe's *El Litoral*, to name just a few.

The Spanish sports newspaper *Marca* published his profile, along with an extensive interview, which was unexpectedly popular. Two radio stations, one from Barcelona and the other from Andalucía, would be the first in Spain to broadcast the footballer's tendencies as a dreamer, and dozens of Argentinian stations also contacted him. The globalisation of internet communication contributed to the appearance of his name, story and pictures on hundreds of websites.

The grump, part two
On Tuesday 18 January, during the melee produced by the win over Derby County, Crawley

Chapter 7

Town visited Bath City for a league match. The team managed an easy win (2-0), but Sergio, in the middle of his heyday, would experience another one of his frustrating moments.

> *I was playing well during the first half. I took a shot with my left foot from just outside the box, but I hit it wrong and the manager started yelling at me like mad. I thought that would be it, but at half-time, after entering the dressing room, he came directly over to me and, with an ugly look on his face, yelled: 'What are you thinking shooting from there?! Who do you think you are?! Just because you scored against Derby you think that now you can shoot from anywhere?!'*

Paisa kept his mouth shut, not understanding why it was necessary to reproach him so much in front of everyone.

> *I was putting up with an unpleasant lecture just for having taken a shot.*

His team-mates backed him up and told him not to worry about the yelling, and that it was because the manager just thought he was acting like a prima donna. Despite their comforting words, his blood was boiling. The next Monday he went to the manager's office amid tension.

"Do you have some sort of personal problem with me?"
"Me?"
"Yes, you."
"Why do you say that?"
"Because I don't feel I'm being treated right. You always yell at me and it makes me think you don't like me."
"You're right. I don't like you ... I love you!"

He told me he loved me and gave me a hug. I didn't know what to do. I had to laugh, but at least I let him know I don't like the way he talks to me.

That beautiful, little ball

Torquay United would be visiting Crawley for the fourth round of the FA Cup. The golden hand had returned and was prepared to continue writing about the club's unprecedented success. The match-up was admittedly tough, but a win wasn't out of the question considering the previous win over Derby County. After all, Torquay were in League 2, only one division above Crawley.

The meeting would turn out well. With a Matthew Tubbs goal in the first half, a tumultuous second half (two penalties awarded to Crawley, but both missed), the usual ravings of the manager and a bit of luck, the Reds found themselves heading for the fifth round. The team went nuts

Chapter 7

in the locker room, and the media continued its frenzy.

The staircase, which had seemed short at first, had steps appearing out of nowhere. It was unexpected for Paisa, having dropped down several levels, to be experiencing his best year as a professional footballer. He had been injury-free and he was playing in almost every match, standing out against teams from the Conference, League 2, League 1 (Swindon Town) and the Championship (Derby County). Furthermore, as if all that wasn't enough, there were still more surprises waiting around the corner. The draw for the next round of the FA Cup was to be held the day after the 1-0 win over Torquay.

> *Lena wanted to go to the shops in the centre, so I went with her. We were inside one and I was looking at my phone to try to catch the draw online, but I couldn't get a signal. I went outside and saw a television shop across the street. I told Lena that I was going there to see the draw and that I'd be back. When I went in, it wasn't playing on any of the screens. I asked the salesman to do me the favour of changing the channel and he asked why. I told him I played for Crawley Town.*

When the man in the shop changed the channel, there were only a few balls left, and among them was the '1', Crawley's number. There was a mix of emotions that were growing without explanation. Any result really was a positive one. Slowly, more people started coming over to see how the draw would turn out and some just out of curiosity. There were dozens of people in front of the television, gathered around the curly-haired guy who was staring at the screen in obvious expectation.

> *Manchester United's ball dropped and I got even more nervous. Suddenly, the people doing the draw started to laugh. I was shaking nervously, and then out came number one. I almost died. I started jumping around and shouting and everybody looked at me as if I was mad, but I didn't care. I kept yelling and jumping and went over to bear hug the TV salesman.*

Another of his life's dreams would be coming true: playing against Manchester United, in a competitive game, at the magical Old Trafford. His uncontrollable imagination had prevailed against common sense and he was headed to the Theatre of Dreams.

> *Dad, you're going to have to come back to England, no matter what. How many times are you going to be able to watch your son play at Old Trafford?*

Chapter 7

The heart beats nervously
Before coming up against Manchester United, Crawley had three important league matches. The last two were against Wrexham (one at home and one away), a team also fighting for promotion to League 2. The second would be played on 15 February, only four days before the most important day in the club's history.

> *It's probably the only game ever that I've thought, 'well, if I don't get to play today, no problem'.*

Sergio was worried about injuring himself and was finding it difficult to focus during the matches. There were only two words running through his brain: Manchester United. The squad, however, would do its best to forget about the future and ended up putting on a great display in both games versus Wrexham. In the first, they were losing 2-0 but they came back to win 3-2. The next match was also well fought and ended a 0-0 draw. That day, there was a special guest in the stands, watching Crawley Town with interest. Months earlier, who would have expected to see Sir Alex Ferguson in that stadium?

Saturday 19 February was the date circled on the calendar. The Thursday before, the squad had travelled to Manchester having been seen off enthusiastically by their fans. That same day, they would visit the impressive stadium for the first time.

> *I took my video camera and regular camera. I looked like a tourist, but whatever, it could be my only opportunity to do that, and I wanted to take advantage. The manager wanted us to feel the grass under our feet so we wouldn't be so nervous later.*

The following day, the 18th, was the final training session, but it didn't turn out so great. Unexpectedly, just when everything was going so well, a bit of misfortune would strike.

During a training drill of attack v defence, something happened that Paisa would love to be able to go back in time and erase. He got the ball, passed one defender, the ball got away from him and, when he went after it, he nailed Kyle McFadzean in the left ankle with his cleats. The defender fell down screaming in pain. Steve Evans blew up at the Argentinian, yelled at him a while and threw him out of the practice. 'You're a fucking clown!' was the manager's phrase of choice for the situation.

> *Steve was telling me that now Kyle wouldn't be able to play and asked me how I could do something like that the day before the match. I was praying he would get up and that it would*

Chapter 7

stop hurting. While I was walking off the pitch, I felt the world closing in on me. Now I won't play tomorrow. He's going to drop me. I'm an idiot. How could I do such a thing? I've been trying so hard not to injure myself and now I'm not going to play because I hurt him unintentionally.

Everybody around saw him on the verge of tears as he was walking away. He stayed strong and avoided letting them flow, but the knot in his throat was choking him.

Pablo Mills, the captain, tried to defend the Argentinian, who finally was able to calm down a bit when he saw Kyle McFadzean up and moving around with the others (his sock was torn and there were cleat marks on his ankle).

I tried to explain that it had been an accident and that I would never do something to hurt a team-mate, but the manager wouldn't listen. Finally, three or four minutes later, he called me over and put me back on the attacking team. I was frightened. I didn't even want to see the ball or run around, in fear of touching somebody, and this led to me making mistake after mistake with the ball. At the end of practice, I apologised to Kyle a thousand times. He knew it had been an accident.

The Sergio Torres Story

Already in his room at the hotel, Sergio continued thinking about the unfortunate incident during training. The only thing he wanted to do the night before the most important match of his life was rest, but it was difficult. The nerves, the anxiety and the fear of not being in the starting 11, due to the manager's aggravation, were keeping him awake.

> *I was begging my head to let me sleep, please. I was worried about it, and remembered the problems I had experienced when I played for Peterborough, when my troubled mind barely let me get a wink. I thought about taking something but, as I had never done it before and didn't know how it would affect me the following day, I decided against it. Ben Smith, aka 'Smudge', who I was sharing the room with, was sleeping like a baby, breathing deeply, and this bothered me even more. I think it took me about an hour and a half of tossing and turning before I finally fell asleep. At 6:20am I woke up and I couldn't get back to sleep. I couldn't stop thinking about the day, the match, how the stadium would be, and so on. Smudge woke up at 8:30am and we went to breakfast. The first thing I did was ask Kyle how he was, and I was thankful to hear that it wasn't bothering him much and that he would be able to play with no problems.*

Chapter 7

Steve Evans had said that he would announce the starting line-up after breakfast, before leaving for the stadium. So, after filling their bellies, the squad stayed in the dining room waiting for their manager to arrive and tell them who would be the 11 men starting the match at Old Trafford.

> *When he came into the room, he told me 'Serg, come here', and took me to the room next door. My heart started pounding. He called me over and took me to the other room to talk alone! I thought I wasn't going to play. My world was crumbling to pieces. Why else would he call me aside, in front of everybody? It has to be because I'm not starting.*
> *It's obvious.*

"Do you know why I want to speak with you alone?"

"Don't tell me I'm sitting on the bench, please. Don't tell me that."

"What?"

"Don't tell me I'm sitting on the bench," he repeated on the verge of tears. "I'm asking you, please."

"Definitely not. You're one of my most important players. Forget about what I told you yesterday. You know me. I'm pulling you aside to tell you that I want you to walk into that game and be the best player on the pitch. I want you to do today what you did yesterday to Kyle."

"OK, boss."

In the first person

On the Thursday afternoon, my father and his friend, Alberto 'El Colorado' Ciardi, arrived in London. My old man didn't want to miss the match because it would be his only chance to see his son play at Old Trafford. I didn't want him to miss it either so I paid his way. My uncle Pepe (José Torres) and his son, my cousin Leandro, also came along. They had been looking forward to coming to Europe and were starting with a visit to England to see me.

For the match, I decided to give tickets to the people that had helped me the most. I invited John and Mimi, but only John could come, as they are living in France now. He was super happy. I also invited Keith, my supervisor from Boots, and Lena's father and brother, who came from Germany. My friend Lucas Sotelo and his cousin Matías came from Spain, where they have been living for something like ten years. Pezza also made the trip, accompanied by his friend Ben Spooner, who gave me a nice gift. He designed some special boots just for the match – red and white, the team's colours – which said "Sergio Torres 8" on one of them, and "Paisa Torres 8" on the other.

Chapter 7

I saw my dad on the match day. I spotted him during the warm-up and waved to him from the pitch. He was wearing his attention-grabbing orange cap, which he has worn to every game of mine since I was little and playing in Mar del Plata and even now in England. He also brought the big flag with "El Coyunco" written across it, which he had problems getting through security. They told him not to open it or they would throw him out. In his stubbornness, he wanted to take it out, and he did one time. But later, Lena was able to convince him to not do it again.

After giving us the line-up, the manager allowed us ten minutes to call our families. "Good luck, baby," were Lena's words. "Play relaxed, as if you were in El Coyunco. Don't worry, everything will be great," my father said. I told them I was super nervous and that I'd never felt that way before. Very, very nervous. I normally get anxious before games, and I hate the hour leading up to the start of a game. I would prefer to arrive and start playing, without the warm-up, but you can't do that. The adrenaline flowing through my veins that day was totally different. This was authentic nervousness.

We started the trip from the hotel to the stadium and, before arriving, we could see fans from both sides walking along with their team shirts, hats and flags. There were 10,000 Crawley fans. It was incredible. When we got off the bus, they all greeted us. There were a lot of people around. I felt like a real star.

The stands started filling up little by little and we went into the dressing room for last-minute preparations. I have a few rituals. I always tape up my ankles, first the right, then the left. I do the same with my socks, shin pads and boots, first right, then left. I also dampen my hair, throw cold water in my face and slap myself a few times.

The manager said some final words and we went out to wait in the famous tunnel. We were stopped there next to Manchester United's players looking down the Old Trafford tunnel that is so full of history. I had already dreamt of that moment and it turned out exactly the same. We started walking, each player holding a child's hand, and when we entered the pitch it was: "Wooow." The stands were packed. Lots of things came to mind in those ten seconds. I remembered the guys from Cameroon, the failed trials, working at Boots, my mum and my sister, who were in Mar del Plata watching the match on TV (yelling and crying for sure), and I thought of my friends who had got together to see it. All my hard work has been worth it. I had thought that playing at Stamford Bridge would be as good as it was going to get for me, and I remembered my father's words when he told me: "This should help you keep moving ahead and accomplish more things. Don't think that this is it." He was right.

Chapter 7

A lot of things were running through my head until my team-mate Daniel Bulman distracted me. He was behind me in line and started to yell: "I'm so happy, I'm so happy, I'm so happy!" He's a character, always smiling and in a good mood. I turned around and started laughing. I told him: "Bully, don't do that." My head was racing and I was trying to concentrate, and I had this clown behind me yelling and laughing like mad. He's great.

When the whistle blew, I forgot about everything. I don't know how I did it but not one time did I stop to stare at the stands. It was 90 minutes at full gas. We started the match a little scared of them, but we settled down and played our best football in the second half. Unfortunately, we were already losing 1-0 at the time, thanks to a header by Wes Brown.

I was running around like a wildman in the middle without touching the ball much, as they had it most of the time. I was mainly marking the Brazilian Anderson. He's quick and strong, and is quite skilled with the ball. Luckily, they took him off at half-time because of a minor injury, but Wayne Rooney was his replacement.

We came out in the new half with a different mindset. I started to get the ball more and I felt good. At one point, Rooney and I had a 50/50 and we fought it out hard, shoulder to shoulder. Believe it or not, I didn't back down, and I won

The Sergio Torres Story

the ball. "I just won the ball against Rooney," I told myself, smiling inside. I stole the ball from him and I was lucky enough that, at that moment, someone took a picture. I have it in my living room at home and I look at it every day, still hardly able to believe it.

I held on to the ball and advanced. I passed one opponent, then another, then the ball got away from me. Rafael, one of the twins, was coming at me and I knew he was going to get there first, so I laid down a good tackle and took him down. We had had a confrontation in the friendly when I was playing for Peterborough, and that's why I didn't hesitate a moment to get him good. The challenge earned me a yellow card.

We continued moving the ball around well and pressuring. Crawley Town, the little team from the Conference, was putting pressure on Manchester United! We had a clear opportunity to equalise in injury time. Richard Brodie sent in a nice header but it hit the crossbar. The referee blew the final whistle and a mix of emotions came over me; a combination of sadness and happiness. We were only two or three centimetres from another amazing feat, but we had to be proud of ourselves for playing neck and neck with one of the best teams in the world.

After signing a few autographs for the Manchester United fans, who also congratulated us a lot, I headed for the dressing room. On the way,

Chapter 7

with my head down, I was sure I would never be back there. When I was passing midfield, I bent down and tore out a chunk of grass. I put it into my sock as a souvenir, to remember the magnificent day. I did it carefully so nobody would notice, looking all around in one big motion. I found out later that more than a million people in the world saw me. The television cameras caught me and, if that wasn't enough, all of the newspapers published a picture of me with the piece of grass in my hand.

Outside the stadium, everyone was waiting for me: my friends, the pregnant Lena, my father, my uncle and my cousin. I talked to my mother and sister on the phone and they were incredibly thrilled. In that moment, I understood that the result didn't matter. I had won, and I received possibly the best recognition of all: my dad gave me a huge hug and told me he was very proud of me.

The never-ending wheel of dreams
* On 9 April 2011, for the first time in the club's history, Crawley Town won promotion to League 2, the fourth tier of English football. Sergio Torres was one of the squad's main figures, scoring four goals in 39 matches (34 as a starter). Crawley finished the season as champions, with a record-breaking 105 points, bettering Aldershot's total of 101 from 2007/2008. They also played an

amazing 31 consecutive matches without losing (another record) and tied the record for fewest losses in a season (three). Also during that time, they were the only club in the top five divisions of English football to not lose a game by more than one goal.

* On 7 June 2011, Luna, a beautiful baby girl, was born to Lena Schlee and Sergio Torres, in Kamen, Germany.

* Keith, Paisa's former supervisor at Boots, retired. He now enjoys spending time with his family and continues to attend the Basingstoke matches on Saturdays. They are still friends.

* Mimi and John live in France and have three gorgeous daughters: Madeleine, Celestine and Eugenie.

* Jorge Timoner, Sergio's former agent, who provided him with a place to live after he was kicked out of Roland's house, is working for a German bank in Hong Kong.

* Mike Williamson, his room-mate during his first night as a professional footballer with Wycombe Wanderers, is currently playing with Newcastle United in the Premier League.

Chapter 7

* Russell Martin, Sergio's team-mate at Wycombe and Peterborough, and his former flatmate, is a key player with Norwich City in the Premier League, and plays for the Scottish national team. After a match against Manchester City, Martin asked the outstanding Argentinian striker, Sergio Agüero, for his shirt to give to his friend. Russell married Jasmine, and they have a boy called Reno.

* Cristian Levis lives in Spain with his girlfriend; the one he met when the two boys were playing together. He manages a youth team for a club based in the Basque Country, Elgoibar FC. He had to stop playing after suffering several knee injuries.

* Claire, his 'little sister' from High Wycombe, is already 12. She would love to be a veterinarian and also is a swimming fanatic, a sport in which she started competitively when she was eight. She also likes singing.

* John Gorman, the manager who gave Sergio his professional football debut, has recovered from the deep depression caused by the death of his wife. He published his autobiography in 2008, which talks about how he got through that tough time and how it left an invisible and lasting mark on his life. The book also mentions another difficult moment of his life: the tragic accident

which resulted in the death of Wycombe Wanderers' Mark Philo.

* *FourFourTwo* magazine, the prestigious English football publication, named the Argentinian the best foreign player in the history of Crawley Town FC.

* In the 2011/2012 FA Cup, Crawley Town, again, surprised the football world by reaching the fifth round of the tournament for the second consecutive year. They were beaten 2-0 by Stoke City.

* Sergio maintains a good relationship with Rob Fisher, the psychologist, who later admitted to him: "I had a problem similar to yours but I wasn't as strong as you, and that's why I didn't recover."

* On 5 May 2012, Crawley Town obtained their second consecutive promotion, reaching League 1, the English third division. After 46 matches, they earned 84 points, enough for third place, nine points behind Swindon Town and four behind Shrewsbury. It was Sergio's third promotion in England and he had contributed as a stand-out member of the squad, playing in 38 games (37 as a starter) and scoring three goals.

Chapter 7

* On 1 June 2012, he married Lena in Germany and later, on 23 June, they were married again in Argentina.

* He is still waiting for Carlos Tevez's shirt.

Just one question
During one of the thousands of conversations held while this book was being written, a simple question was asked…

"Paisa, man, what would you say if, in 20 years, Luna told you that she wanted to go to Japan with 300 dollars in her pocket, without speaking the language, without a place to live, and wanted to fulfil her dream of being a businesswoman in Tokyo?"

"If she says that, I'll tell her there's not a chance: 'You're staying here with us until you're at least 25.'"

ABOUT THE AUTHORS

Sergio Torres
Born in Mar del Plata, Sergio is not one of the most important and influential players in world football. Neither has he won a World Cup. But he is a footballer, a scorer of goals, who has played as an amateur or professionally for Quilmes de Mar del Plata, Banfield de Mar del Plata, Deportivo Madryn, Molesey, Basingstoke Town, Wycombe Wanderers, Peterborough United, Lincoln City and Crawley Town. He dreams …

Twitter: @Sergio_Torres08

Juan Manuel López
Born in Buenos Aires, Juan Manuel López is not one of the most important and influential figures in world literature. Neither has he won the Nobel Prize for Literature. He is a journalist and writer who worked for the newspaper *El Clarin* from 2006–2013. He has written books on the centenary of San Lorenzo and Huracan, published by Grupo Clarin, and was editor of the special magazine *El Grafico*. He also dreams …

email: jmlopez_85@hotmail.com

Printed by Libri Plureos GmbH in Hamburg, Germany